THE LOWER LEVELS OF PRAYER

1957

THE LOWER LEVELS
OF PRAYER

BY

GEORGE S. STEWART, D.D.

" *Do you make a place in your daily life for inward retirement and waiting upon God, that you may learn the full meaning of prayer and the joy of communion with Him? And do you live in daily dependence upon His help and guidance?* "

—Society of Friends' Queries.

LONDON
STUDENT CHRISTIAN MOVEMENT PRESS
58 BLOOMSBURY STREET, W.C.1

First Published   July 1939
Second Edition March 1940
Reprinted   February 1952

PRINTED IN GREAT BRITAIN BY
LOWE AND BRYDONE (PRINTERS) LIMITED, LONDON, N.W.10

CONTENTS

A PERSONAL FOREWORD

THIS book is dedicated very gratefully to my wife and daughter, by whose love my life is made glad.

It is about the lower levels of prayer. There are higher levels of prayer than it speaks of, and those who walk there are not likely to find anything of help here. Many books, ancient and modern, describe these higher levels, and tell of the disciplines of mind and spirit which help men to rise to these. I write of simple ways of prayer, open to folk of no special spiritual endowment, and which bring life to real communion with God.

The book is addressed to those who find prayer *in its continuance* a difficult thing and are not satisfied with the place it has in life. It does not attempt to deal with speculative difficulties, vital as these are, but with the practical difficulties of keeping interest fresh, of finding deliverance from distraction, of bringing vitality into what is at times a burdensome devotional exercise.

It is assumed that for many people prayer is an exercise of the soul which demands training and discipline; that it is a difficult thing to learn to pray and that many need guidance in the ways of prayer.

It is assumed that helpful ways of prayer can be taught, and that earnest people are willing to give time and energy to learning these, as in trying to learn a language, an art, a science. This book aims at giving some help in this and is written in the belief that such help may be more acceptable if given on the lower levels of devotion by one who is himself trying to learn, than if given by a master of prayer, who is walking on a different plane.

It assumes that even in our confused prayers the Holy God is acting and that the divine movement, the supernatural grace, is the one effective element in what we call *our* praying. It is God's response, and it alone has merit and saving power. We seek to open our hearts to God, and there is no action of ours by the merit of which the response of His grace is regulated, an action which we may call a prayer of faith, a good prayer. There is the reality of our need, we with our sins and ignorances and longings, our wrong ideas, our faiths and fears. There is the Holy Father God, revealed in Jesus Christ as loving just such men, all men, " God so loved the world ". How can the response of such a God be regulated by the quality of our praying?

Therefore, all that is written here about method and plan, expression and thought, discipline and custom, is not to acquire merit in praying, but to bring sensitiveness to the supernatural grace, the response of God.

It is assumed, on every page, and as fundamental to every opinion or claim, that *God is a seeking God*, whose love watches for any movement of man's spirit towards Him and responds to that. He responds to ignorant, stained, superstitious, blundering prayers of blinded men with all His energy of love, watching that He, Seeker of the Souls of Men, Shepherd of Lost Sheep, may find something to lay hold on with saving purpose. Every word of this book is written in that belief, as distinct from any teaching which requires of prayer some excellence in itself before God makes response.

Doubtless it will contain expressions which are inconsistent with this view of prayer, and the emphasis on the lesser things will also seem inconsistent. The subject and its relationships are too large for strict consistency, on my level of thought—yet this is the fundamental belief underlying the whole.

The book is concerned solely with individual prayer, a great limitation of the subject which the necessities of space demand. It also must omit the relationship between prayer and Scripture, which is so vital.

One of the difficulties in writing about the subject is that the book may be read by those of very diverse experiences and temperaments. What is acceptable as a method to one, may be felt as unreal and crippling to another. What helps one in October when the freshness of the summer holiday has not departed, may be a harmful load in March when the strain of a winter's work has affected life. I shall try to state the principle on which each practice spoken of depends, but the personal element is the finally determining thing. This personal element itself is not constant. Someone has said, " I should know myself better if there were not so many of me." We need to keep this in mind, lest we try to force a practice or a response which is not helpful to the " Me " who is dominant at the time. Nothing in outward practice is inevitable or constant although it may be very regular. The end of study, experiment, practice aimed at is that each individual may *know how to pray in his own way*, the way in which he finds fullest response to the presence of God. This way may be very unconventional and apart from the manner in which others pray. The one test of value is real communion with God.

This book includes an article published in the

International Review of Missions, and most of the substance of a little pamphlet on Prayer published by the Church of Scotland. At the time of publication, arrangements were made for re-issue of these in book form and I am grateful to those concerned for their approval.

I should be more than ungrateful if I did not here express my great debt to two young friends, the Misses Betty Whitehead and Nettie Martin, who, from interest in the subject and desire to help in the publication of the book, have given up many long evenings to copying out rough drafts and revisions, and have greatly lightened my work.

In Scotland still the first teaching about prayer which most children receive is through a catechism born in Westminster but only at home in the sterner north.

"Prayer is an offering up of our desires unto God, for things agreeable to His Will, in the name of Christ, with confession of our sins, and thankful acknowledgment of His mercies." (Shorter Catechism, Q. 98.)

It is a good beginning to practical theology.

G.S.S.

CHAPTER I

GENERAL THOUGHTS ON PRAYER

" First of all, my child, worship and adore God, think
of Him magnificently, speak of Him reverently, magnify
His providence, adore His power, frequent His service,
and pray unto Him frequently and constantly."
—LAW's *Serious Call*—Paternus to his son.

PRAYER and common life are vitally connected.
There are certain acts in life which we rightly
consider as specially religious, prayer, worship,
Bible-reading, and others. All of these as definite
acts are occasional, however regular. Although the
spirit of prayer and of worship abide in the heart,
as definite acts they do not occupy the greater part
of our life, yet life is directed by them. In these
acts the great battles of life are fought and the
great fountains of joy and peace spring up. Life,
on the other hand, directs these, and what we call
our common life fills these acts with penitence and
thanksgiving and the whole content of experience.
So life provides a critical estimate of the reality

17

and sincerity of these specially religious acts, while they in turn open a new vision of all that ordinary life can attain.

Our life is very largely, so far as it is of importance, a matter of human relationships. Whatever our day's occupation is, the day is well or ill lived according to these. The only real progress is progress there. All kinds of work are judged by their value to men, "By this shall all men know that ye are my disciples, when ye love one another"—that is, by your relationships. Prayer and this point of common life are, above all other spheres, interactive, for only through prayer do our lives enter into the deepest communion with men and with God. Here again life is a sign of how we pray.

Some reader may object to the matter in this book because it presents for prayer a great claim on time and attention. I assent to the criticism that it does make this great claim. I should be ashamed if it did not. There is room for a reminder that a description of any act of prayer may be far longer than the act itself. The actual requirement of one minute in prayer may here take many pages, to show its principles, its necessity, its bearing on other parts of life. While that is true, the demand is there. I should be ashamed to write anything which suggested that prayer was an easy thing using up odd moments only. Yet I should be as much ashamed to write anything which suggested that a man is shut out from ample entrance into prayer, when our complex civilization has so gripped him that the energies of brain and muscle and spirit are exhausted and his time filled full of necessary toil. Few actually are in such circumstances, though many think they are, but when that state is real for a man, *all values of time and mental powers are transformed for him* if he has the will to pray; yes, even if he falls asleep at his prayers. For him, also, there are special usages, full of grace and of miracle for him, but not for anyone who would try to make them a short cut to a life which demands more than he is willing to give.

It is not likely that any will be turned to prayer by lessening the demand it makes on life. It makes no unreasonable demand, when its magnificence is seen.

It is necessary to remember here that prayer holds two elements. There is quiet communion which rests and refreshes. When the mind is weary God's communion does not increase its burden, when the spirit is worn God's communion does not bring any deepened strain. This is the prayer of rest, not a prayer for rest but a communion which refreshes and restores. It is well that all kinds of prayer should contain this turning to God in silent, adoring communion.

There is other prayer which draws upon the mind and the will, and is intensely active. In it is found the battlefield of life. This book speaks specially of such prayer. You will not think it false to what is written here of the necessity of such active prayer if I remind you in this introductory chapter that there may come times when there is real nervous and spiritual exhaustion. The signs of these are very often a refusal to stop working and a determination to fulfil our plans even if they deepen our inward weariness. Quite definitely then the more active part of prayer, its energy of thought and search, should be given up until refreshing has come to body and mind.

This is a good time to use books of prayers, when with no special energy of will or resolve the mind can hold its doors open towards God through these prayers which have come from the heart of other men. We recognize that life is a unity of body and spirit, and that prayer is not a substitute for ordinary common sense in dealing with these. It is a way of attaining common sense and guidance in every part of life.

Great part of the so called spiritual worries of devout souls comes from want of recognition of the fact that life is thus one and indivisible. The poisoning of some disordered organ is mistaken for blameworthy spiritual decline, and excited nervous conditions are mistaken for visions and revelations of the Lord. People think they have grown cold and lost their love for God when they are just very tired, and should go to sleep or take a holiday. There is a world of wisdom in the humour which dictated a sentence in a little medical dictionary published some years ago: "Biliousness:—an affection of the liver *frequently mistaken for piety.*" Spiritual life is nourished by a wisely ordered breakfast as well as by a chapter of Thomas à Kempis. Life is one. Spiritual life is not a mode of living but the essential quality of our being, and all our activities, mental and physical, and all our passivities affect it, and are dictated by it.

Recognizing fully the bodily conditions under which we live and their legitimate demands, the assertion remains that there is a supernatural bestowal which changes these conditions and brings them into a much more healthy relationship with all life. All work and all life is dependent on this spiritual gift, and it has prayer as one main channel of its entrance. It is the gift of a life, constantly renewed, and developing the whole being of him who prays. Everything is brought into keener and deeper life by communion with God.

It follows from this that there is no need for the most overworked person to fear that there is not time for regular and leisurely waiting upon God. Literally, it saves time. All life is affected, and every power of it, memory, reason, judgment, will, discrimination, is quickened. With the calmness and strength which communion with God gives, even manual labour is less exhausting. "I can do all things through Christ who strengtheneth me," said St. Paul. "All things are possible to him that believeth," said the Lord Jesus. There is no loss in the day's reckoning when time is taken to hold communion with God about it.

When habits of life are changed so as to give fully separated time for prayer, there may be at first a real lessening of work, at any rate it will be felt as real. I would press the fact that it is only apparent. It is undoubted that this communion with God, learned and practised at set times and in disciplined ways, continues as an undercurrent of all life, as the waters on which life flows, and it greatly affects the ordinary limitations of time, space and energy. Take as example the life of a doctor, with many calls on his time. If he takes time in his day to get into communion with God, if he uses the means of grace known and approved as channels of God's incoming, till he is "set in God", he will be as regularly swifter in diagnosis, surer and steadier in operation, more calm and decided in judgment, less wearied by the unreason of his patients, and the drudgery of the day. He will day by day do more work in bulk and better work in quality and come less weary to the end of the day, and he will leave a deeper revelation of God on the lives of his patients, than if he rushed to his work without this preparation, so as to have an hour longer to do it in.

If you take it merely from the physical and the psychological sides, any first year medical student can tell why this should be so, but there is another element than those which science knows. There is some prevailing influence from Him who healed all who came to Him. The same principle applies to workers at all kinds of tasks, students, housewives, nurses, business men, all.

There is no loss of time, there is no giving up of work, this is the way to do the most work and the best, for life is quickened and quietened at the same time, and there is given much more than compensating energy. *To make time for prayer is to save time for work.*

The same thing applies to the time of prayer itself. In response to its needs the ordinary limitations of time tend to expand, if not to disappear.

We know that a dream which holds sequences of action and experience covering long spaces of time is often contained in a few moments. There is the old stock saying that a drowning man may have long periods of his life passing before him in a flash. Whether that be so or no, such an abolition of the conditions of time does take place in communion with God, and a very few minutes may hold a far longer and deeper content than ordinary thought or converse could experience in the same time. This heightening of the speed of the faculties is particularly noticeable when the usual longer and appointed time for prayer becomes on special occasions impossible and the few minutes are approached with confidence that our restriction to them is according to the will of God, with whom "One day is as a thousand years and a thousand years as one day". The illusion of time and space is matter for very interesting speculation, but we can experience that about which scientists and philosophers discuss. We ordinary folk may find the reality in prayer. The tyranny of time and space are overcome when we, to use the mystic's phrase, "Sink to the ground of our being, in God", and are faithful in prayer.

CHAPTER II

ON SETTING ONESELF TO PRAY

AT times we do not set ourselves to pray, but turn eagerly to God, even if with stumbling words and confused desires and thoughts. Whether we be driven by love for others or by joy or need or sorrow, these are likely to be times of real communion and response. Perhaps the saints of God pray like this all the time, finding intense communion, as when lovers speak with one another or in silence are satisfied.

On lower levels this is not constant, and the attempt to act as if it were opens the door to wandering thoughts and desires. The driving impulse is not strong enough to keep the mind closed against other interests. We kneel to pray and find ourselves composing a letter or planning some work or dwelling on some grievance—or at any rate, not praying.

Against this lower experience there is a measure of protection in " setting ourselves " to pray, with a definite way arranged, a sequence of thought and expression and will, even with prepared words if these be found helpful. This is not only a measure of protection but a wise means of widening the area and deepening the content of our regular prayers. When we are under strong compulsion or emotion, prayer is usually somewhat narrow in its range. Such prayers need to be supplemented by more expansive if less intense thought and communion.

It would seem wise that our devotions should range along a wide and far-reaching orbit of prayer. Especially in thanksgiving and prayer for others width of view liberates the spirit from dwelling exclusively on our own immediate conditions. There is always a whole world for which to make intercession, a world in which God is working and in which we can see His glory. When we turn from the thought of that to our own special interest, some of the glory has spilled over on it and hope is stronger.

So also is it wise that the stated prayers follow a course which is ordered in independence of any one mood or experience. These will, of course, enter into it largely; but even a broken-hearted man is better to have a definite place for thanksgiving, and a joyful man for the sorrows of the world, taking them upon his heart. This dictates a definite sequence in prayer, whatever the mood.

AN INSTRUCTION IN ONE WAY OF PRAYER

(Altered from a pamphlet written for the Church of Scotland)

When we set aside a time for prayer, whether that be long or short, and seek to have in it such practices and follow such principles as will most readily bring us into communion with God, common sense and ordinary courtesy suggest six natural steps:

1. Closing the door on other pursuits, interests, attractions of the mind.
2. Regarding in reverence the God whom we thus approach.
3. Thinking of the matters which we wish to bring before Him.
4. Speaking of those.
5. Accepting His response.
6. A reverent withdrawal from that special interview.

If only five minutes can be given to this, or five hours, these hold as sensible and courteous. There are sudden cries of the heart, and times and tides of devotional feeling, or of devotional reasoning, which do not follow this outlined path. These break into life on occasions, or these colour and shape the whole texture of life, but they usually have their roots in the more determined and regularly appointed "prayer times" of the day. These prayer times cannot omit, without loss of valuable elements, any of the things detailed above. At first they are deliberate and may be formal; later, they are the natural sequence. In describing them the word "kneel" is used. That means, "Take your habitual attitude of prayer." Some stand in preference to kneeling. Some clasp their hands only. Where prayer has to be in a public place, an unobtrusive action is necessary. All this is included in the word "kneel" in the following description.

Whatever time we assign to our separated prayers and however various the content we put into these it is good that we should approach and end this prayer-time *ceremoniously*. In between, there is place for more free and unrestrained communion.

"Enter into thy closet and shut thy door," says Christ. There may be a good many doors to shut, other than that which keeps spectators away: and I suggest first that the usual attitude of prayer be taken and the mind withdrawn from its hold on anything. This is not an effort so much as a purpose. If made an effort it defeats itself, for the mind is occupied with the effort. Let the will to shut the door be there, and kneel in that purpose: let a moment or two pass. Whatever happens on any one day the purpose and the attitude will form a habit, which really closes the door on many an intrusion. Literally a few seconds, *not more*, is helpful for this.

Then "Set the Lord before you", as the Psalmist says. It is He to whom you will speak. It is His voice you wish to hear. Look then at Him. This is a definite act of the mind. Attach it to some appealing thought of God, His Majesty, His Holiness, His Intimacy of Knowledge, His Love, or to some haunting message or gracious promise, or to some revelation of God in Christ. "I am the Light of the World"—"The Lord is my Shepherd, I shall not want"—The Healing Christ—the Tempted Saviour—Christ Crucified—A Resurrection Scene—The Judge of all the Earth and The Coming of the Son of Man. Look at any such revelation: say over slowly any such message: think of any such aspect of Majesty and Love. In so doing, keep in the foreground of your mind: "It is *He* to whom I am now come—*this God, this very God.*" The wonder of this may so hold you that you cannot turn from it, and your separated time passes before this adoration ends (but we shall not call it adoration just yet). This may rarely or never happen, but you will always pray with a deepening consciousness of God, Very God of Very God, present and interested.

Attach great importance to this as a part of your praying, and call upon Him by the Name which best expresses your vision or thought of Him *at that hour*. It deepens the sense of reality, and gives the ground of hope and assurance in praying. It is possible to pray with no such presentation of God to the mind. Such prayer often leaves us unsatisfied and uncertain that any real communion has taken place.

Following this there are many ways that may be taken, Intercession, Thanks, Petition, in any order. Your life will find its own best order, and the order will vary as your experience changes and one mood or one need or one desire predominates. In private prayer there is an unreal element introduced if the dominating desire has to wait expression in conformity with a fixed order, but it is good to have an order which you find *ordinarily* most natural, so that there is no hesitation about what comes next at this separated time.

Whatever act of prayer is in view, *think about it first*. Of course the actual prayer will often far outrun this thought, for prayer awakens and extends every thought and desire, but it is good to begin with quiet consideration. This makes a prepared way, though God is very sure to carry us farther than the desire with which we began.

Begin, say, with thanksgiving. Probably it is

best to rise from kneeling and quietly consider what your special thanksgiving for that day is, the thing that is really in your heart, *or can be put into your heart.* Even if you use a form of thanksgiving or a book of prayers, it is needful to consider its clauses anew and make them live, so that they become really your very own prayers. There are always special things, new experiences, new realizations—the look at God may bring floods of these—old blessings that grow dearer. It is good that the little things of life, as well as the great, should have a place in the thanksgivings, the little things that bring a joyous moment. They will not shut out the great gifts of God which deeper thought and faith unfold.

Then kneel and speak your thanks—coldly if your heart is not warm; dutifully if you cannot lovingly; courteously if that is all you can bring. "Manners maketh man", and this acknowledgment will help to gather fuel, and light the fire of real, loving gratitude. Not many words are needed to express very deep thankfulness.

Perhaps in your order, intercession comes next. Begin again with thought. What are you going to seek, and for whom or for what causes will you pray? What do these need in your judgment? Probably there are some needs already crying in your heart, and some less poignant, which do not

" cry " but are in your memory, and some which a sense of responsibility or Christian feeling keeps you from neglecting. Seek what you really desire for all these.

Petition will possibly come next, but remember that this order is quite likely not your order, it is only an order by way of example. Here, too, the same custom follows. Think first of the needs and desires you wish to bring to God. Then lay them before Him with eagerness and trust. You can be quite sure that God will make response. Watch for it. It may be hidden in some surprising event or in the more humdrum movements of life. The urgent need is to get into communion with God, about every desire of your heart. He who is Guide and Saviour has a way prepared to purify your desires. Bring every desire into your prayers and intercessions. You need not press them on God. "Wrestling in Prayer" does not mean "Wrestling with God". It is yourself you have to wrestle with, and to hold back any desire when you are praying is a hindrance to true life, and gives no help in freeing oneself from tainted or foolish longings for others and yourself.

Confession next?   No.   All your prayers, even your rejoicing and triumphant prayers, will have in them a vein of penitence, a sense of unworthiness, and many a revealing of that will be in your thought and will temper your praying. Specific confession of sins cannot, however, wait for an appointed time. It follows swiftly on the knowledge of transgression, the more swiftly the better. Any act of redress which you can make is more readily offered, and more surely accepted before there is time to brood over it, or absorption in the day's work to reduce a keen regret to a dull uneasiness. Never delay the cry to God for pardon and cleansing.

If some specific commission or neglect breaks into your prayers, the right moment for confession and for beseeching has come, however much this may disturb the planned order.

Accept God's response to your prayers. It is a right and natural thing that all your speech to God should end with some act of the will which opens mind and spirit to any response from Him. One of the chief avenues for this response is in the will which accepts it, while seen or yet unseen, and thanks God for this fruit of your prayers.

A reverent close. This belongs, perhaps, less to the essence of prayer than to the psychological technique which helps in praying. Outwardly it consists in finishing your prayers, spending a minute in silence as at the beginning and then slowly rising from your knees, or unclasping your hands, or passing out from the place of prayer. It may seem an artificial thing, but actually it does a good deal to affect the "set" of the soul. The slow, lingering withdrawal from the attitude of prayer has a calming influence on the multitude of other interests that stand ready to invade your mind. You carry the atmosphere of the upper chamber away with you. This is what a wise teacher, Dean Goulburn, says about it: "When we have withdrawn into ourselves for a while for communion with God, the glare of the world should be let in gradually on the mind again. The impression of having had an interview with the King of Kings should not be tossed off, but gently and thoughtfully cherished. And it shall be as a nosegay of fresh flowers, which a man gathers before he leaves some fair and quiet garden, a refreshment amidst the dust and turmoil of earthly pursuits." (*Thoughts on Personal Religion.*)

The description of this sequence of prayer has taken a good deal of space. This prayer-time itself will occupy just the time we wish to give it. Ten minutes is not too short for real prayer in this order, though a longer time is better. All our prayers cannot be gathered into this time, but the progression in it can be continued at other times. It is full of vital activity.

Here in a short space are certain definite

features. There is the worship of the body, the willed and enforced *attitude* of prayer. There are acts of *recollection* in which we review the mercies of God, the needs of our friends, our own needs. There are acts of *discrimination* by which we choose out of a whole world of impressions those most vital for our communion with God. There are acts of *devotion* in which we bring to God recollections and thoughts and choices and speak to Him of them, with gratitude and desire. There are willed *acts of love*, more or less emotionally real, but real in will, in which we bear before God the need of others. There is *expectancy*.

This cannot go on day after day without the soul growing sensitive to divine influences, the mind swift in apprehension, the will steady in obedience.

So this time of prayer seems to end, but there is no act of prayer which does not pass into a state of desire which dominates life and conduct. We see people and things in the common ways as we looked on them in our prayers, often a greatly changed vision. There is no clause, say, of the Lord's Prayer, which does not in a very ordinary Christian life, pass into a continual desire and attitude of the soul to God, to which other things are subordinated. Do not confuse remembrance of the state of the heart and soul with the state itself.

Our minds may be much taken up with common work and intercourse and our thoughts centred in the act of the moment, without the loyalty of our wills and hearts being in the slightest degree diverted from its object in God Himself.

A mother may be absorbed in some household or social duty, but that does not affect her unceasing love for her child, her permanent state and loyalty and her continual desire. Not even unconsciousness in sleep can affect that, or check it—

> "In a mother undefiled
> Prayer goeth on in sleep, as true
> And ceaseless as the pulses do."

Penitence, Thanksgiving, Longing, Intercession, all the acts of our communion with God, have their value in so far as they pass into states of heart and will. If they are sincere, they deepen and improve the state they spring from. Love as a state of the soul is strengthened by generous acts and words in which it reveals itself, and so it grows able for more generous acts of its outpouring, these two acting and reacting to more and more perfectness. So is it with the state of love and trust we call Prayer. The word of prayer is less really true unless some state of prayer underlies it, but again the word of prayer is a mighty power to deepen and purify the state.

This state of the soul towards God and the interests of His kingdom is that which the apostle Paul invites the Thessalonian Church to enter, saying to them, " Pray without ceasing. In everything give thanks."

Conscious remembrance or thought, much less conscious speaking, cannot be " without ceasing " in our life. This continual " awareness " is normal in Christian life, and it is kept so by regular prayer, even prayer on these lower levels.

CHAPTER III

THERE is prayer at times set apart, and there is sudden prayer in the midst of all sorts of circumstances and at all times. This latter is of necessity short and direct, usually with one definite intention, and it is called in the literature of the subject ejaculatory prayer, that is the "javelin" prayer, the prayer thrown. "Bring me my arrows of desire," Blake says. This is one of the most important parts of prayer, so long as it is associated not only with a cry of desire but with an act of will. Common life is full of calls for such prayer, thanksgiving for the beauties and goodness of life, intercession for the continuous procession of needs that cross the daily path, invocations which are thrown from our hearts not at set periods but in the business and distraction of human life.

Where laziness or lack of disciplined life or fear keeps us from observing the longer and more deliberate periods of prayer, this swift and unstudied prayer is likely to die or to become mechanical and unmeaning. Where it rests on a life which is making serious response to the claims of God it becomes one of the most inevitable and vital ways of prayer, because it is a most vital way of living. There is no area of life which it does not invade, and there is no area of prayer which it does not enter. Deliberately set before us, it may begin as a practice of prayer which seems unreal, but it deepens into true communion and into the sense of God's interest in all common things. It is obvious from the older books of Celtic devotion that this practice has been fostered by forms of prayer, familiar and of daily use, associated with the humblest acts and incidents of common life. There are prayers on drawing the nets, on sweeping the house, on covering the peat fire for the night, before milking, before baking, and so on through the common daily acts.

On Lighting the Lamp

Mother: God be thanked, now we have light.
Response by family: May the Lamb of God
   bring us all to the light of Heaven.

This intimacy of prayer is partly the result and partly the cause of the extraordinarily vivid sense of God's presence which still distinguishes Gaelic prayers. Such prayer feeds the longer and appointed times, for it brings into consciousness much that otherwise would pass unseen in the life of the streets, the needs of men, the manifestations of God in human life.

When Making a Bed

This bed I make
In the Name of the Father, and of the Son,
    and of the Holy Ghost;
In the name of the night we were conceived;
In the name of the day we were baptized;
In the name of every night, every day, every
    season,
And of every angel that is in Heaven.

(An interesting collection of these is published by Messrs. Sands & Co. *Prayers of the Gael*, by R. MacCrocaigh.)

It is a good spiritual exercise to walk along a familiar street with the eyes directed toward successive aspects of those things we can most readily imagine our Lord seeing there.

We may take this walk looking for the signs of God's presence as that is represented in human life. We may look at the children's play, at young people in the joy of their love, at parents proud of their children; we may listen to happy laughter

and happy song; we may note the beauty of colour
and form in such a thing as a fruit-shop window;
we may see men going out to their day's duty or
returning with their duty done; we may note the
fullness of service of God's world represented by
public vehicles, by the shops and by the count-
less activities of industry, and praise God for it
all.

So again we may walk seeking to see the need
of the streets. There will be needs that we cannot relieve, there will be needs we could relieve
easily but to which we have been blind, and needs
that we could relieve only at great cost. We will
see the need which owes its persistence to the fact
that we with others have not sought to undo a
wrong. As we walk we try to imagine what our
Lord would Himself have done in each case that
our eyes fall on, and try to learn what He would
have us do, and as we walk we ask God for His
blessing on all.

So, selecting now this and now that aspect of
life, we may take many such walks in busy streets
or in country lanes. Every journey in 'bus or tram,
every railway station, every church or meeting-
place, provides a point of observation. All life
does. We connect this with prayer, seeing what
to give thanks for, and those to make intercession
for, and again where we need forgiveness, and all

c

in connection with which we may offer ourselves to God.

Our tendency is to get so accustomed to the things our eyes are often seeing that they lose their meaning, and we miss God in them. In addition to this more general temptation there is a temptation to encourage blindness, and " pass by on the other side ". On our way through the day we often have our goal before us and on our way thither ignore the casual call from the wayside, yet the casual may be the more important. We acquire thus a sort of protective mimicry which disguises our walk as that of a blind and deaf man, lest any show of our sympathy should demand of us action which we do not then care to take, but for which no other time will serve.

In recollection we may now and then ask ourselves what emotion has chiefly dominated our ejaculation-prayer; gratitude, pity, penitence, responsive interest. It is possible for three common men to see the same incident; say a very poor child caring tenderly for a young brother, and be affected respectively by differing emotions — thanksgiving, penitence and compassionate intercession. What would the characteristic predominance of each emotion tell about the normal prayer life of each man? Such a look at ourselves may be a helpful revelation, but like all introspection it should be infrequent. Infrequent, but thorough when it is done.

It is obvious that these swift and immediate prayers, and the vision which calls them forth, depend on a state of life which is in habitual communion with God, and looks on the world with the eyes of Christ, and this does not seem to belong to the lower levels of prayer, nor to be the ordinary life of ordinary folk. To set our feet on the way does, however, so belong. To take such a walk, deliberately, with calculating mind, and watchful eyes, may be far removed from the gracious life which does not need deliberation, but it is part of a training in vision. To make a deliberate resolve to approach certain actions in life, beginning a study hour, paying a visit, leaving or entering the home, opening the shop or office door, meeting a friend, with a swift prayer to be kept in communion with God, is not the same thing as the joyous sense of His constant presence, but it is on the way to it. To speak in the heart a benediction for someone as we pass, may readily become an unmeaning formula, but it may as readily become an increasing energy of love, a real gift.

"The Lord be with you." Even as a friendly wish this is worth while, but our Lord's teaching implies a reality beyond a kindly wish, it is *the bestowal of a grace.*

When a benediction is pronounced does any thing happen? If a Church service close otherwise is it poorer? If we bless a friend in the name of the Lord is it more than a religious-sounding expression of goodwill, a somewhat pious form of "The best of luck"? During the Great War I went into one house where a young fellow was sleeping by the fire, half drunk, and on his way to the station for embarkment to France. His sister, whose house it was, told me the condition he was in. I had prayer before leaving the home and spoke a blessing on the sleeping man, who was going back into the dreadful night. A week later the sister came to tell me that he had been killed, and said, "I feel so thankful that *you put a blessing on him* before he went away." Has that any reality of meaning? If we visualize "the grace of the Lord Jesus Christ, the Love of God and the communion of the Holy Spirit" in some form which appeals to the immediate senses, may we expect to see these graces descending and resting upon all, when the usual benediction in church is spoken?

This "resting upon all" is what actually happens. It happens even to the careless. To those who stand expecting to receive, a blessing is more real than any material thing, as the spiritual is ever more real.

In reading the ancient liturgies, one is impressed with the large place which is given to the " Blessing of the Congregation ". It is much more varied than with us and much more frequent. A few from these early forms are given here. Each one of these is prefaced by a prayer which seeks for the blessing, which through the messenger of the Lord is then given. There are scores of such forms. Mostly they are threefold, and the congregation responds with " Amen " at the end of each. For our private use they may act as guiding our desires and deepening their urgency.

Ancient Benedictions

(Extracted, with grateful acknowledgments, from a large number in Plummer's " Devotions from Ancient and Mediæval Sources.")

1. May the Lord Jesus Christ, who is the Splendour of the eternal Light, remove from your hearts the darkness of night. Amen.

   May He drive far from you the snares of the crafty enemy, and ever set to guard you the Angel of light. Amen.

   That ye may rise to your morning praises, kept safe in Him, in whom consists all the fullness of your salvation. Amen.

2. May the Lord bless you, and protect you with His own Right Hand. Amen.

May He deliver you from all temptations of this life, and pour the grace of His Holy Spirit into your hearts. Amen.

May He take away from you every stain of sin, and lead you to the splendour of all His Saints. Amen.

3. May the Lord our God hear you, and favourably look on every one who calls to Him in need. Amen.

May He graciously grant the solace which human weakness needs, and avert the sins which oppose you. Amen.

And may He ever grant you all things profitable, both for your souls and bodies. Amen.

4. May the Almighty bless you from on high. Amen.

May He look upon your labour with a favourable countenance, and hear your petitions with a pitying ear. Amen.

May He make your work well pleasing to Himself, and preserve your life in holiness and peace. Amen.

CHAPTER IV

" One way to recollect the mind easily in the time of prayer, and to preserve it more in tranquillity, is not to let it wander too far at other times."
        —*The Practice of the Presence of God.*

O WISE Brother Lawrence!

A business man begins to seek God's guidance and suddenly finds that his mind is composing a letter or following some transaction instead of praying. A housewife is offering her thanks or her petition, and the details of the spring house-cleaning or of household management keep breaking in. The parent prays for the children and the mind flies off to some memory or desire, and prayer is interrupted. Sometimes also direct evils invade prayer, a quarrel, a letter which stirs resentment, a haunting temptation. All this is true not only of private prayer but of listening to and joining in the prayers of the church. This latter is indeed a difficult spiritual exercise, needing more preparation than it usually gets. There is a technique of prayerful listening which it is good for worshippers to learn.

Distraction in prayer is not altogether a bad thing. There is much to be learned from it. The frank recognition of it is good, and wisdom in dealing with it, such as God promises to those who seek, brings wisdom in dealing with many other activities of life and thought.

Perhaps our first consideration should be given to an attempt to ascertain the sources of distraction. Then we can pay heed to those things in ourselves which open the door to it. Distractions have much to teach us about ourselves. Probably the deepest analysis would say that they are due to lack of faith and to a will imperfectly yielded to God. This is perhaps true, but it is not the most immediately helpful analysis. There are certain things which lie nearer the surface, which have to be taken into account if our prayers for this deeper faith and this more consecrated will are to be unhindered.

Distractions are often the natural consequence of an imperfectly disciplined mental and spiritual life, or of habitual separation between prayer and common life. There may be at the time of praying lack of vital interest in that for which prayer is offered, often due to some unconscious doubt of the value of prayer in bringing real help.

They are at times instruments of the wisdom of God calling us away from our other prayers to deal in prayer with the emotion or need which disturbs. On the other hand distractions are an element in the constant warfare of man's life with these forces, mysterious and apparently so personal in their attack, which invade our quiet hours, and disturb our active efforts as disciples of Christ.

Whatever be the cause of distractions it is wise that they should be dealt with *without depression or self-blaming*, seeing in them signs of our own imperfection or sin, and learning through them to recognize our own need, and the voice of God, and the places of the Enemy's approach.

Lack of discipline

We are the same people when we are praying and worshipping as when we are doing anything else. Our nature and mental processes do not change when we begin to pray—they may have much changed before we finish, by the goodness of God giving new steadfastness, new grace, new love. We carry into our praying just the kind of persons we are, our common ordinary life. Whatever has urgency in our habitual thought or frequency in our dreamy meditations will break into our praying.

A disciplined life in any sphere is a life trained to attend to the matter engaged in, and it is to be sought in every part of life or it will not be permanent in any one part. If we are easily distracted in life, we shall be easily distracted in prayer. Very specially is it to be sought in our special communion with God, for here the *gift* of more disciplined earnestness is given and *the gift is not for that hour alone, it is a gift for life.*

So we use the common-sense ways which lead to controlled thought and spirit. We set aside our time for separated devotions and keep it. We appoint some order of our reading. We follow an order of our intercessions, not letting that become a prison but using it for guidance. We recognize a place for confession and thanksgiving and all the divisions of prayer, using the recognized principles of an ordered life which proceeds from point to point. This is learning to pray as much as praying, but there is need to learn, and the foundation principles of all learning are the same; " order, closeness of attention, gradualness ". There is no means of strengthening these in other departments of life which it is not legitimate and right to use in connection with our praying—pen and pencil, plan and programme, rule and correction. It is through this common door of learning that many come to a life of prayer where these as conscious

acts are set aside and we can hold unhindered communion with God.

Most likely this arrangement of thought and
the sense of progression will shut out some distractions. Some of them will enter, changed. The
joyous excitement which unsettled us becomes a
part of thanksgiving. The sorrow or fear which
disturbed us adds earnestness to our petitions. The
injury or annoyance enters into our prayers as
intercession for him who did us wrong, or becomes
a part of our penitence for our own evil. When
we can make our distractions become vital parts
of our prayers, they are no longer hindrances but
spiritual influences of good.

This perhaps needs a word more for those whose
temperament and training make steady progressive
thought or prayer very difficult, perhaps impossible.
It is good to accept the fact without being down-
cast about it, and to do what can be done to improve the condition, without judging your own
prayers as worthless because they are spasmodic
and broken. They are your prayers, and God does
not need a perfect expression of the heart's desire.
It is God to whom we come and in whom we trust,
not in the quality of our prayers and the steadiness
of our minds. One whose thought is disjointed,
and whose mind is easily turned from subject to
subject, cannot pray *in the same way* as one with

a disciplined mind, tenacious in following one line of interest, but the prayers may be as full of loving desire. We pray in accordance with our own natures to a God who understands and sees the heart.

For those of all temperaments and training, however, there is help to be gained through the arrangement of thought, and of progression from one state of prayer to another. The mind helps the spirit and even directs the emotions. Many distractions are shut out by the regular progression, such as is detailed in Chapter II.

Another cause of distraction of a lesser kind is that we sometimes come to our prayers hurriedly, and, plunging into them too swiftly, trail with us the affairs of the day. There may come a time when there is no veil between the prayer periods and ordinary living, but on the lower levels the veil is still there and we have to pass from one state to the other. So long as that is so, it is wise to take a minute or two to " settle ourselves " before we speak or read. We seek to gain a sense of entering a place of audience, a chamber of the King. Even to sit quite quietly or kneel with nothing but the attitude of devotion or stand with clasped hands has an effect on the restless mind or the dull, uninterested mind.

Lack of interest at the time of praying

This does not imply that there is no vital interest or that there may not be a constant deep undercurrent of it, and on occasion great emotional outflow. Probably, however, there is no interest of our living, not even the love for our dearest or a great and sorrowful need, which does not vary greatly in its appeal for attention.

It helps to keep our interest throbbing if we have in our prayers large adventurous desires as well as intimate requests. Many a " little " prayer becomes uninteresting because of its fitting into the ordinary framework of the day's life, and the need of prayer is not obvious. The great impossible things, which only God can effect—these keep their sense of wonder and awe. They are ventures of faith, and a venture always keeps interest alive. Our Lord incites to such prayer. " Ask whatsoever you will, and it shall be done unto you." " Whatsoever ye shall ask in my Name, that will I do." " Hitherto have ye asked nothing in my Name, ask and ye shall receive, that your joy may be fulfilled." His teaching is full of this, in words which seem denied by experience. St. Paul felt this denial, but as he realized the power of the grace of God in the human soul, he learned to pray " impossible " prayers and to rejoice that even his most impossibly great were within the limitless purpose of God's Will. So his extravagant desires end in a cry of triumphant praise.

"I bow my knees unto the Father, from whom every family in heaven and on earth is named, that he would grant you according to the riches of his glory, that ye may be strengthened with power through his Spirit in the inward man; that Christ may dwell in your hearts through faith; to the end that ye, being rooted and grounded in love, may be strong to apprehend with all the saints what is the breadth and length and height and depth, and to know the love of Christ which passeth knowledge, that ye may be filled unto all the fullness of God.

"*Now unto him that is able to do exceeding abundantly above all that we ask or think, according to the power that worketh in us, unto him be the glory in the church and in Christ Jesus unto all generations for ever and ever.*"

(Eph. iii. 14-21.)

In these words, as intercession for others, or as petition for ourselves, every clause seems wildly impossible: "filled with all the fullness of God"! And yet, and yet—do they not stir a longing and waken a hidden hope, as lesser prayers do not? Pray like that and triumph. "Prayer turns the

tread of half-beaten men into the march of con-
querors."

In the whole range of life great prayers arouse
great interest. We feel, quite wrongly, that we can
manage so many of the little things without prayer,
using only a little more watchfulness, a stronger
resolve, or some human effort. This saps interest.
We must keep up the little intimate prayers also,
the more intimate the better, and these, set against
the background of the great desire, reveal themselves in their real dimensions. They are not little,
but urgent acts in our relationship with man and
God.

Immediate interest is kept alive by deliberate
watch on the outcome of our prayers, so far as these
can be traced. "The Lord working with them, and
confirming the word by the signs that followed"
(Mark xvi. 20), applies to honest praying as fully as
to honest preaching, imperfect though the praying
and the preaching be. There are signs following,
and to watch for these and see them means that
we come to our prayers with fresh interest and
hope, or it may be with more trouble of mind and
perplexity of spirit. In either case there is life and
interest, not a saying of words to which we expect
so little response that we do not watch for it.

> " 'Tis ye, 'tis your estrangèd faces,
>   That miss the many-splendoured thing."

Watchfulness brings interest. It reveals that something is actually taking place *in connection with*, if not in direct answer to our prayers.

Interest is kept from dulling into listlessness by increased knowledge. Where prayers are for peoples and causes somewhat remote from our daily lives, other nations in distress, overseas missions, groups of people, poor people, unemployed, patients in hospitals, sailors and fishermen, miners and so on, the vastness of the area tends to reduce interest and invite wandering of the mind. This vastness is the opposite of the vastness of request, the "venture" which increases interest. This is more fully considered in the chapter on Intercession, but these points may be mentioned here. (1) Prayer of this kind must grow in knowledge if interest is to be sustained. There are always sources of knowledge available, and to pray without seeking to learn about that for which one prays inevitably results in decline of interest. (2) The prayer for a group of people can centre in an individual or individuals more intimately known, with prayer that God will extend the blessing to all in the group, and assurance that God's response is not limited to those whom we are able to name. (3) Interest is kept alive by some service or giving for those who are held in our prayers. This may be money, or a vote in their interest, or other personal service. There is often something we can do in friendship or sympathy, and interest is kept alive.

Probably it is better not to pray concerning that in which we have little interest, for we cannot hold everything in our prayers, yet it is well to remember that prayer is a well-spring of interest in all that is dear to God.

Distracting thoughts may have their source in God

We recognize that many distractions and wandering thoughts have their source in some evil, even if that be only our own weakness. Yet we do well to watch among them for the Voice of God. If any seemingly alien thought comes in at a time of prayer it may be wise to ignore and suppress it. Sometimes it may be even more wise to accept it, lift it from being a wandering thought into our prayers, deal with it before God, and then go on at liberty. Such is usually wise when it is some thought of disagreement, or sense of wrong done or received, or any fear. We watch the distracting thoughts which are most persistent, for God may be revealing through them our real need and disturbing our plan and rule for His finer ends.

God responds *to the person praying*, always and in love, not only to the petitions. This seems to make it inevitable that often the prayer being offered will be pushed aside by God and the spirit called to face His call to some more urgent thing. So persistently our prayers are invaded by something we need to face; a personal relationship, a call to do, or to abstain from doing, an uneasiness. Perhaps some who read this may know what it means to pray and rise from the knees swiftly, lest God should respond by revealing His Will with greater insistence, and show a clear issue of obedience or disobedience. We do not wish to face, on that level, all that is in our prayers. Many men have ceased to pray for a time, lest God should then have a better opportunity to make His Will clearly known.

In face of such intrusions into our prayers there is only one reasonable course. We must face them, hiding nothing, evading nothing, and when God's Will is plain, conforming to it at once. There is neither peace nor joy in our praying if it be detached deliberately from any part of life.

In prayer we " fight against a living enemy "

Beyond the needs detailed above, and our consideration of how to meet them, we have to remember that there is in life a disturbing and distracting element which specially attacks all our " holy things ". We have often to pray against an inner opposition. Conceive of that as we will, our own indolence, ignorance, sensual nature, earthliness, there is deep and long continued opposition to our communion with God. As a working hypothesis, I find nothing so fits all the experience as does the conception that we " fight against a living enemy ". " Our wrestling is not against flesh and blood, but against the principalities, against the powers, against the world-rulers of this darkness, against the spiritual hosts of wickedness in the heavenly places " (Eph. vi. 12). Very old-fashioned, no doubt, very primitive! Very unmodern! We have learned psychology since St. Paul wrote and our Lord spoke! We know all about complexes and obsessions and the subconscious and the sub-subconscious!

No theory denies the fact, the experience and the mystery of it. Prayer is often dry and difficult, and there is opposition to our praying. Our task is to meet this opposition with courage and without depression even if we cannot reach to undisturbed prayer or thought. The desire which we would bring to God, the search for closer communion with Him, the obedience to the duty of penitence and the joy of thanksgiving, the purpose of bearing the yoke of Christ and sharing His intercession are frustrated and broken in our thought and our utterance and our emotion. Yet they are all bringing response from God, deeply affecting ourselves, and blessed for the service of the world.

" Blessed for the service of the world "—for it is the sin of the world as well as our own which thus assails us in our prayers. Hear this very wise voice which comes to us from the fourteenth century.

> " It happens sometimes that when one is pray-ing for the same person, one occasion will find him in such light, and holy desire before God that the soul (of him who prays) will seem to fatten on his welfare; and on another occasion thou shalt find him when his soul seems so far from God and full of shadows and temptations, that it *is toil to whoso prays for him to hold him in God's presence.* . . . His soul will have stayed sterile, dry and full of pain—which God makes that soul which is praying for him perceive, and God does this in mercy to that soul which re-ceives the prayer, that thou mayest aid Him to scatter the cloud " (Catherine of Benincase, about A.D. 1377).

" It is toil to hold him in God's presence," that is, difficult to pray for him, because of the dryness of his spiritual life. May this not be the cause of some of our difficulties in intercession? In face of the sin and need of the world it cannot be an easy thing to " hold the world in God's presence ", and we are hindered by distractions of many kinds springing from sin, as we seek " to aid Him to scatter the cloud ".

CHAPTER V

THANKSGIVING AND GRATITUDE

" A light came into the world—not a light shed from without, but a light that burns within the heart of the world itself, transfiguring the whole length and breadth of existence, from what it seems to be to the eye of sense into the fulness of its reality—the fitting abode of immortal and rejoicing spirits, the Father's house of many mansions where music and dancing await the regenerated soul, NOT ONLY THE MUSIC TO WHICH WE LISTEN, BUT THE DANCING WHICH REPRODUCES THE MUSIC IN THE TOTAL MOVEMENT OF OUR LIVES."

—DR. JACK'S *The Lost Radiance of the Christian Religion.*

THANKSGIVING would seem to be one of the most natural and inevitable acts of our praying, yet no part is more readily affected by our moods and passing experiences. There is frequent need to remind ourselves that gratitude is something deeper than the emotion of gratitude, and is a principle of the Christian life. Sermons about thanksgiving are innumerable, but it is usually assumed, in defiance of experience, that none of us needs any help in preserving the " principle " of gratitude in our prayers and developing such habits as give thanksgiving a constant and assured place there.

By what method is it attained and strengthened? One does not like to speak of method in connection with this relationship to God. We suspect a grace that needs to be cultivated, that has in it anything not purely natural and spontaneous. That suspicion is wise, if we remember we are dealing with a fallen human nature. In few people is gratitude wholly and regularly spontaneous. Any method is good which helps us to see the goodness of God more clearly and keep it in grateful memory and present trust and future hope.

1. It is wise to keep a regular and inviolable place for thanksgiving in the daily prayers, whatever our mood or experience. If our emotion is intractable, or dull, a form of thanksgiving to which we have given assent in happier days, and which our reasonable mind approves can be used. It may be untrue to our passing mood and wholly true in our will and principle of life, and as we express it on that deeper level it commonly invades the dullness of spirit and changes it.

2. Beyond this, the place for thanksgiving should contain a deliberate recalling of details, and some note of these in permanent form helps to make this regular. Day after day one can set down say

three instances of God's goodness, the lesser incidental gifts, the great and continuous realities of
His grace. There is no labour in this, a single line
or a single word is sufficient for recall, but a Book
of Remembrance is built up. If that seems too
elementary some more worthy " Memorial " can
be instituted.

A general sense of God's goodness and a general
and heartfelt acknowledgment of it are both
deepened in flavour and widened in outlook by
such deliberate noting of details, by memory kept
in good repair, and by some memorial to ensure
remembrance. The Bible history of God's leading
is full of instances of " memorials " of deliverance
being established, and rings with the repeated cry,
" See that ye forget not." Our Lord established
in the Church the greatest of all these. " This do
—in remembrance of Me." There are great pre-
cedents to our having some evergrowing Book of
Remembrance in which is set down part of God's
goodness to us. Out of this, as out of each day's
common life, we feed our gratitude in preparation
for thanksgiving. Can we always trust our
memories? And if at any time we get so lost in
" wonder, love and praise " as we read in it, that
the time for the uttered prayer is very brief, all the
weight of the absorbed mind and heart will be in
the shortest word. If, on the other hand, no emo-

tion of gratitude rises up, there is always the principle of gratitude to guide and inspire our offering of thanks. A faithful adherence to that principle is a way to kindle emotion and to make clear the vision of God's goodness. Emotion often kindles at remembrances of God's goodness, but even if the flame of emotion burn low, reasoned and grounded virtues grow where that goodness is kept steadily in remembrance.

3. Looking over such a note at appointed intervals, say on a certain Sunday in each month, is likely to be a revealing thing. It contains for the most part the things which first start to our mind as we think of God's goodness. These, of course, do not always represent our deeper thought or faith, but the record is certainly of the things most prominent at the time. Later examination may reveal that we are dwelling most regularly among the more material sources of joy, or that these homely things have no place in our first impulses of gratitude. In either case we have guidance for a wider range of thanksgiving. Beyond that, the recalling of the month's (or the year's) outstanding benefits is like walking through a field rich with fair flowers and happy with the songs of God's messengers.

4. Thankfulness depends largely on our use of the gifts, whether these be grace, or daily bread,

pardon or bodily healing. In these uses there is
one of which we are often a little shy. We hesitate
to use them to the full limit of enjoyment and
satisfaction which they hold. Surely it is obvious
that they are meant for use. It hinders gratitude
if we grow suspicious of life's joyous receivings of
God's goodness, and receive everything, even our
salvation, with restraint. The joy of life and its
beauty and light and movement and music are
not tasted to the full. There is no need for this
fear when thanksgiving is in the heart. We need
not hesitate to enjoy the gifts of God, till we have
to sing "my cup overflows". Enjoying their use,
with thanksgiving, runs parallel to using them to
the glory of God. It is in this joy that we can most
truly bring the gift into the service of Christ and
use it in His spirit, without which use every gift
becomes stagnant and corrupt. We are recipients
of God's bounty, gathering it up joyfully and
kneeling with the richness of it before Christ,
that we and it may be in His Will.

5. The last words indicate another practice of
gratitude which keeps its flame alight. It flickers
and dies without this oil. It affects every part of
our praying, but most markedly enters into our
thanksgiving. Oblation is a word which has
largely dropped out of the language of devotion.
It is difficult to put any word in its place, and it

represents a real transaction between God and man in prayer. In thanksgiving we look at the good of life; the "all" for which we give thanks, or some special detail. We next speak our thanks to God. Then follows the Oblation. We take all this good from God, joy, satisfaction, material benefits, spiritual benefits, all He has given, and offer it back to God that it may be serviceable as He wills. The old language said, "Cast it at the Redeemer's feet." (Think over that phrase.) Inevitably the spirit of life which does this brings vision of such uses of our Good, and goods, as deepen their value and blesses others. God responds by showing means to use it all.

So with our intercessions: we offer ourselves at the close of these, in hope, perhaps in fear, but always in obedience, so that God may use us as messengers for bearing His response to our prayers if that be His Will. Whether it be with hope or with fear, we can do this in the obedience which has its roots below such emotions.

So with our petitions: naming to God our needs, and seeing even dimly what would come to our life if these needs were supplied, *we take that enriched life as by faith we see it*, and offer it to God for the purpose of His Will, and so we can ask these petitions—"For Jesus' sake" and "In the Name of Jesus".

We thank God, for example, for a happy and comfortable home. What is the natural sequence to this thanksgiving, either as resolve or as instinctive response? Is it not to take our part in the sacrifices of love which are needed in every home for the guarding of its joy, and also to set the home at Christ's service? Our thankfulness for the gift calls us to ever deepening resolve that the gift be kept unspotted and used in the spirit of Christ. Our devout fathers would have said, that even its furniture must be " marked by the blood of Jesus ". This seems now a strange alien expression, but just think what it means. It means the realization that nothing of this home would be here for us (a plain matter of fact), if Jesus Christ had not died. It means also that when we possess the home in the same spirit as led Him to the Cross, it becomes not a dead possession, but a means of grace and salvation in His hands. It opens the door of it, it opens the friendship of it, to some who else were not welcome.

Accepting a general practice of this kind, it becomes one of the interests of life to watch the finger of God pointing out its application through the events of the day. Perhaps we see some part of that at the very moment of our praying: and resolve and thanksgiving are simultaneous. More widely, as we keep in our hearts the sense of God's goodness, life becomes full of the opportunity to use His gifts, and in using them to find our joy increase.

6. The habit of grateful enjoyment is also our help in a strange and unsuspected place of inconsistent living. Acceptance is not always an easy thing. *In this sphere it is sometimes very difficult.* Gifts material and spiritual are asked from God and gifts are held out to us. Often, however, we cannot accept the very gift we have asked for, except by turning out of our life something which does not leave room for the gift to come in. This may be very hard to do, for this "something" has its place in our lives and affections, and claims its position. It needs new grace if we are to accept many of God's gifts to us, and we receive this grace most readily when thanksgiving is a normal action in life.

7. Thanksgiving and intercession are brethren, and one depends on the other. I once brought relief to an African woman from a sore disease, and when she left for home she kissed my hand and before I could prevent her, stooped down and kissed my feet, and went away rejoicing. Two weeks later a wagon drove into the yard drawn by sixteen oxen, and loaded with sick and suffering people, men, women, children, who had come three days' journey at her report and testimony.

In gratitude she would share a blessing which she had received. This is a parable. It is not when we know that God *can* do certain things, but when our lives are glowing because He has done them in our sight that our prayers for others glow also.

> " Then with a rush the intolerable craving
> Shivers throughout me like a trumpet-call;
> Oh to save these! to perish for their saving,
> Die for their life, be offered for them all."

We are scarcely likely to have passion and thrill in asking for others those blessings of which we have had poor realization in our own lives, or which are with us only as a far off and dull memory; we may not even have dutifulness to ask at all. We are scarcely likely to have faith and confidence in pleading the need of others before God unless we know Him as near and loving, through our own gathered experience of Him. This experience we may have, and yet forget and grow cold. Make much of thanksgiving. We may come to an end of confession, many as our sins are. We shall never come to an end of thanksgiving, for God's blessings are the outpourings of infinite, eternal love.

The sense of our own benefit and the joy of it deepen keenness of desire and purpose towards those who are deprived of good or refuse it. All our thanksgiving, recorded or no, is not only a part of triumphant prayer, but a way of intercession and an inspiration to action.

CHAPTER VI

" And I added another resolve—to be as wide open
towards people and their need as I am towards God.
Windows open outward as well as upward! Windows
especially open downward where people need most."
—LOMBACH, *Letters by a Modern Mystic*.

IN intercession we take on us the Yoke of Christ
and seek to share His life-work and to pray in
union with the motives of His dying, the need of
men and the glory of God. If our intercessions are
to be a real sharing of the work of Christ they
demand earnestness of will and openness to His
Spirit and love for others. " Take my yoke upon
you," " Love one another," " Thou shalt love the
Lord thy God with all thy heart and with all thy
soul and with all thy mind, and thou shalt love
thy neighbour as thyself." These are the guiding
words for our intercession. And if we do not love
like that? Well—if we love anyone, or care for
anyone, or have pity towards anyone, if we even
have some vague idea that God would have men

pray for others and that He, in some vague way, responds—that is our *place of beginning*.

We can only pray as we believe, but our prayers have power and are honest beyond our known belief. In us all there is probably belief in God deeper than we recognize, and as we follow a traditional custom of prayer, we—the children of our fathers—have in our spirits *an undercurrent of faith which is our heritage*. "God of our fathers, who keepest faith with them that sleep in the dust of the earth." This from a Jewish prayer points to part of our heritage. Ancestral faith is personal faith to most of us, in some depth of our spirits.

We desire to help others and so we pray for them. Who are they? This is often determined by our hearing of some special need, and we pray for those who are bearing this, or working to give help in it. Vital and loving desire is likely to bring earnestness of prayer here—a real help when help is needed. Many of our intercessions, however, if we are taking on us the Yoke of Christ, will lie outside that area of appealing need, and here we are in danger from two sides. We may miss wide areas of interests very dear to the heart of Christ, where our help is needed, or we may "take on" so many interests dear to the heart of Christ that we grow burdened and confused by the

E

number of names and "causes". In this latter
case prayers have little love to wing them and little
knowledge to make them interesting and vital.
Such prayer on a lower level is not to be despised
as a step on the way. The mere remembrance and
mention of the names before God is a real act of
prayer, even if only a general and unmoving desire
is in it. It is the recognition of a service one should
give to the world, and an attempt to fulfil it, on the
level of love on which we stand at that hour. As
we learn to know God better the level of love will
rise.

*An instruction for any who need it on preparing
    the way*

I suggest a method, realizing that methods may
become ensnaring and mechanical, and yet believing that here—as in every other department of life
—they more usually bring liberty and completeness.

The first step is to answer the question, "Whom
shall I hold in my regular prayer?" (This is apart
from the appeal of special and often temporary
need mentioned above.)

The answer to this should be *written just as it
rises in the mind*, for that order gives, even if not
exactly, the place that the names hold in your
interest, or affection, or estimate of need. Do not

press this into a hunt for names of those whom you might help, and yet unite with the names which spring forth some others given to your memory by a sense of duty or responsibility. Some of these may personally be distasteful to you at this stage, but you wish them well. Can you put in the names of some who have wronged you? Try to do it. It is an adventure in prayer: *and they must be brought in sooner or later.*

2. Here then is the list so prepared. The next step, or a prior one, is to decide what time you are able to give to this work for the glory of God. You will probably find that you can give more time on some days than on others. Arrange with this in view, and with consideration that this is a way of help for the world, an urgent and valuable help. Arrange a time which you can reasonably expect to keep, and treat the plan as provisional, but binding till it be deliberately changed. Plan for, say, a month. In actual living all time-measures prove to be different from our view of them as we plan. Usually we cannot put so much into them as we had hoped to do. So it is wise, till experience confirms your planning, to make provisional arrangements.

3. Then you bring these two together. This also is provisional, and it is difficult to do it wisely. There are those whose names will be daily in your

prayers. There are those whose names will be spoken on, say, one day in each week, and others whose names are presented monthly in your prayers. No one can guide you in arranging this. The only advice I can give is that you avoid putting too much into any one period so that the prayers get hurried, that you encourage yourself in the faith that your prayers are giving real help to men, and that you take the next paragraph into consideration as you arrange the list.

It is possible to arrange that people are in your prayers more often than their names are on your lips, if you treat some of the names as representative of a group, and arrange them on that basis. For example: " Charles," whom you know and for whom you would pray, is a doctor, or a man fighting against some temptation or yielding to it, a worker at some dangerous toil, a minister, a teacher, a bereaved friend. You gather round that name others known to you. Beyond that, you take into your thought all doctors, or all tempted folk, all seamen, and so on. You may not wish to call this arranging, prayer, and it is done at all sorts of times in preparation for the special devotional hour, but it is truly prayer. This done, " Charles " still keeps the individual place in your prayers, but he is now also a representative of many others. It may be that as you pray, he alone is in your immediate thought, but many more are in your heart's desire, for you have considered their need with sympathy and united it with that of your special friend. The blessing you have asked for "Charles" is not limited to him. It comes to all known and unknown who are in your real desire, whether they be in your memory at that hour or no. Gradually the impression grows that there is standing round him for whom you pray a company of others whose need unites them to him, some faces clearly seen, some only dim. Their need comes into your prayer. Parents praying for a wayward son are thus praying for all wayward boys. When you hold up the need of this sorrowing friend to God you are holding up the hearts of all sorrowing people. Your intercessions gather round one representative figure, and for the most part, on any one day, details of prayer are associated with him, while the needs of the others are presented in more general terms, but often one or other of these will step into the centre of your thought and desire, as God calls you to share his special need.

4. The next step is to *think over* the need about which you would pray. It has to be taken "on your heart". You would pray, let us say, for our own country. (Of course you can insert here any other name.) Obviously this demands that you think about the needs of Britain. Obviously also

your thought cannot cover all Britain's need, nor can your search or reading ascertain it all, nor can your speech express all that you do know. This inability seems to demand the use of some inclusive word. " Thy Kingdom come, Thy Will be done in Britain as it is in Heaven." " I pray for my own homeland, seeking all that the Lord Jesus seeks for it." Following this constant " all inclusive word " is a varying extension of the prayer for our land, in which now this and now that detail is taken on your heart, and spoken in your prayer. These two fuse together, and the details keep the constant phrase from losing interest, and give to it deepening interest and passion.

For example: every prayer for Britain is gathered up in one special inclusive phrase. Along with that, on one occasion we mention specially the Church, the universities, the schools. Next day the same all-inclusive prayer is used, and also the Government, our own civic government, the courts of justice, and so on, day after day. Some of these details call to penitence for our share in an evil: some call for help which we can give.

Beyond our plan for these details, and often with greater vividness, *there are revelations and calling of the spirit as we pray*. These lead to realization of needs which thought has not reached and quicken the pulses of desire. Here will be found a communion with God about our national need very intimate and moving.

Why, one may ask, may we not trust only in this last way of prayer, entering into immediate communion, without the prescribed thought? Why bring our poor thought to bear on Britain's need when a divine revelation is given?

I dare not say that this can never be done, and I fully believe that on special occasions and emergencies it is the only way to take, and it will always remain as fundamental in our praying that we yield our plan to these " gales of the Spirit ". As confidently would I say that if one attempts to dispense with thought about that for which one prays, and to rely on " immediate knowledge " alone, prayer normally dies for want of food and blood. What is spoken of as our planning and our thought are not " ours " apart from God. There is immediate contact with God in them. We are using the faculties God has set in the constitution of man for communion with Himself and with the world. To ignore them in prayer is not to enter on a higher way but to enter on a maimed life. The authentic voice of the Spirit comes most normally to those who open every door, every faculty, that His every whisper may be heard.

You have " let your requests be made known unto God ". What follows? Silence, if you are wise.

It need not be long, and if it remain just silence,
it must not be long. If intrusive and irrelevant
thoughts come in, it must stop at once. Sometimes, perhaps often, perhaps always, God will
speak, directing you to some action, calling you to
some penitence, opening your eyes to some opportunity, making you face up to some chivalry, invit-
ing you to some thanksgiving or joy—all in connection with your prayer. You will listen to Him
speaking through your reason or in some other
way, and you will listen to Him with at any rate a
desire for obedience, or a desire for desire for
obedience. In the long run, the prayers must be
matched by obedient response to any call of God
in connection with them, and the more whole-
heartedly this is made the more vivid will the
intercessions be. Here too, reason has a great part
to play, for it guards against the fussy kind of
obedience where vision of what needs to be done
for relief or help is confused with a call to do it.
There are services which are not yours, while
prayers concerning them are. It makes prayers a
distracting thing if you associate with every part
of it a *search* for something you may do to forward
the cause, though that is better than the dead praying which never bends in that direction. Yet it
is distracting and may lead to a life of fussy work.
When you come to your prayers, seeking for an

obedient spirit, and having prayed, listen for any call of God; it is God's work to make the call plain, if the task is yours.

Our intercessions begin with those who are dearest to us, but before we end there is intercession for our enemies and the world's enemies. Often these are not really enemies, and there is just some stupid misunderstanding which makes us think of them as such—yet there are real enemies in the world, cruel and selfish men and women. In praying, you will remember what a dreadful thing has come upon them, for every cruel or selfish person has to live always with himself. We should not like to live one hour with him because of the evil in his life. He has to live with himself year after year, and that is a very dreadful thing. We would pray that God would deliver a little child out of such a man's power, and we would gladly serve to set him free, so also we learn to pray that he himself be delivered from himself. He is in far deadlier need than the sufferer, and the remembrance of that helps us to pray.

Pray for enemies, said our Lord. He has not ceased to say it, despite air-raids and poison-gas and submarine warfare. The Psalmists prayed for a curse to fall on their enemies. There is not so much cursing now, and none in our public prayers. We do not sing about it in modern hymns. We speak of these parts of the prophecies and psalms as pre-Christian, and think ourselves above them. So we are, *if we are taking the way of Christ with regard to the enemies of God, not otherwise.* If we just ignore them in our prayers, we would almost (not quite) be better to go back to the hearty cursing of the Psalmists. It, at least, preserved the moral indignation, the hatred of sin, the passion for righteousness which we see in Christ united with a passion of love and pity. We use a very weak substitute if this burning indignation which flings itself cursing on the evil-doer is replaced with anything which does not burn with something like the love of Christ. And the evil-doer needs our prayers more than the sufferer.

This energy of love does not forbid, but demands, passionate prayer that God will cast down from places of power men of injustice and cruelty and greed and will replace them with men of good will. If a nation starts to pray for this the issue will not be long deferred, and we have full personal responsibility for our sharing in the prayer.

Another way of approach to prayer for them is through our desire that Christ should see of the travail of His soul and be satisfied. It is a triumph for Christ when an enemy comes penitent into His

Kingdom. It is such a triumph as this, our Lord tells us, which makes the angels of heaven rejoice. Fix on the worst and most injurious person you know; think what it would mean as witness for the power of the Gospel if he became a true and earnest follower of Jesus; think what it would mean of triumph for our Lord—then it will not be hard to pray for him.

This is one of the places where we learn what a supernatural thing prayer is, and how marvellous is the power of saving grace.

Last of all, match these intercessions with some act of thanksgiving and faith. Indeed it is wise to do this with all prayer. To express your confidence in God, to praise Him for your free access to Him, and for the assurance of response according to His Will—the best experience one can know—this is the natural ending to any time of prayer.

CHAPTER VII

INTERCESSION AND PETITION

THESE two divisions of prayer, so different in their intention and scope, would seem to demand different treatment. In part they do: but since they are both "asking" there are many elements common to both, and in the first place these can be considered together. They both, as does all prayer, have their end in glory to God.

Prayer for others, or Intercession as it is technically named, is asking from God the help they need. This, however, is not all it means. There lies behind it a habit of mind and spirit learned in prayer, and which shapes the requests made. *Intercession is communion with God about others*, seeking to learn God's will for them, and to cooperate with it. Wisdom in asking and eagerness in desire come from this communion with God, and from it also come confidence in asking, and assurance that our prayers have real value, and are active forces in the lives of those for whom we

84

pray. / "I seek this or this for my friend"—that may have much wisdom and vision, but it may also be unwise and impatient so far as the "this that I seek" is concerned. Only the love in the prayer is worth anything then, and it is worth infinitely much, for even when a specific request is short-sighted and unwise, God can translate it into terms of this love, passing by its foolishness. Yet there is disappointment and confusion for us, and a possible weakening of our faith as we see our requests set aside. / We may actually be asking, asking with eager desire, that God will remove a blessing, a purifying influence, a strengthening discipline, a "means of grace" from a friend's life. In real communion with God about our friend we can more fully set our requests within God's will, and if great mystery remains, "In His will is our peace."

This is equally true of our petitions. It is in communion with God about them that they find their purifying and their confidence.

In prayers of intercession or petition it is helpful to single out the prayers we can make with confidence, because they are made "in the name of Christ". In some things we are so sure of His will that we can make prayer with no reserves. / Of such prayers Lady Julian of Norwich said, five hundred and fifty years ago:

" I (God) am the ground of thy beseeching.
First, it is My will that thou have it,
And then I make thee to will it,
And then I make thee to beseech it,
And if thou beseech it, how should it then be that thou
    should not have thy beseeching? "

Thus when we pray for a Christ-like spirit, we
know with assurance that our Lord desires this for
us more than we ourselves do. He is " the ground
of our beseeching ". What disciplines of sorrow
or joy we must receive, what developing experience
we must pass through in preparation for the gift,
we do not know. We do know what Christ's desire
for us is.

We pray for a friend who has fallen into sin : is
Christ with us in desiring his restoring? We pray
for a friend in sorrow : do we believe that Christ
desires his deliverance from its bondage, or from
its circumstance only? We pray that he may be
able to use and offer his sorrow to God. One of the
most terrible things in life is the amount of wasted
and unmeaning sorrow; we pray that he may be
delivered from that : is that Christ's desire? Dealing with prayers in that way, those stand out in
which we have no doubt, as in the Lord's Prayer,
that they are in accordance with Christ's will.
Our prayer in these is not our prayer alone,
tainted by our weakness and coldness. It is His

prayer, even as it rises to our lips.   We can pray it
to God the Father, " for the sake of Jesus Christ.
In the name of Jesus Christ."

Prayers for the spiritual well-being of others,
and for our own, have a new breath of faith and
joy in them when we remember this.   Christ Himself has spoken of doubt about such prayer as a
preposterous thing: " If ye then, being evil, know
how to give good gifts unto your children, how
much more shall your Father which is in Heaven
give the Holy Spirit (Matt. " good things ") to
them that ask Him " (Luke xi. 13).

Confidence in those greatest prayers throws its
influence over all petitions.   The joy of it makes us
ready to come to God with trust about every need,
and mood, and desire, even the smallest want of
life.   We know that He who gives such great
blessings will withhold nothing that is really good
for our friends or for us in our time, and state, and
place.   Also, having learned to trust Him like
that, we learn to hold these other desires with less
eager hands, and to be content with His withholding and His delays.

It is common experience that when prayer has
a full place in life, personal petition grows less and
less and is content with a simple, wide grouping of
requests.

While petition almost invariably grows less, we

lose something valuable if we accept the teaching that it is the least valuable and indeed a somewhat sordid part of our praying.

Objections are sometimes raised to petition and even to intercession on the ground that a real Christian is content to leave all things in the hands of the God of Love. "Prayer should be thanksgiving and adoration, not a beggar's approach to God." At first sight this does seem a high degree of Christian trust. There are two definite points of opposition to it. The first is that it shows ignorance of human nature, the second is that it affects to be wiser than Christ, whose own prayers had in them definite requests, and who counselled His followers to pray with definite requests, urging this upon them with emphatic teaching and great richness of promise. He bade them persist in their requests even when it seemed as if God did not wish to grant them. In St. Luke xi and xviii we have parables to that end—two startling parables. While it is true and right that personal petition grows less in proportion to prayer for others and to thanksgiving, both of these are emptied of some of their content if petition dies away. We thank God for petition granted with a more grateful sense of His intimate care than when the need is supplied before we realize its presence. For others we seek more eagerly blessings of all kinds, material and spiritual, when these are such as we ask for ourselves and the value of which we know.

The chief difficulty about intercession lies in hesitancy as to its value, a hesitancy which often falls into such doubt or denial as makes prayer impossible. The same is true about petition. The frequency and the paralysing effect of this are real in a wide and unsuspected area, both with regard to the prayers of the Church and to men's individual prayers.

We have a friend who has gone to another land, and about whom we now know only this, that he is in a dangerous area, that he finds new habits and circumstances disturbing to his faith in God, that letters can no longer reach him. We know that we could help him if we were with him, and that we have helped him in the past by our letters. Can we effectively help him now by our prayers? On the honest answer to such a question the vitality of all our prayers, not only of our intercessions, depends. It brings our belief in a relationship with God through prayer to its simplest terms. If our answer is " Yes ", even if we add " Help thou mine unbelief ", we are accepting *the fact of divine responsive action, independent of human agency, on which all prayer finally depends.*

I have no evidence to offer beyond the religious interpretation of history, the example and instruc-

F

tion of our Lord, the revelation He gave of the Heavenly Father, and the testimony of those who have been so helped. These are sufficient to give vigour to an assertion that every earnest act of intercession affects the situation towards which it is directed so vitally as to create a new situation. Through it circumstances are often changed, and even if these are unchanged hearts are changed, and when hearts are changed circumstances are transformed, till temptations become altar stairs, and a cross becomes a gate into life. No situation remains the same when prayer is made about it. There are influences of many kinds, good and evil, operating in every cause and in every soul, and each of these has power as an element in the battle between good and evil, but the decisive and essential factor in each case is the loving power of God called forth, or rather made way for, by the intercessions and prayers of Christian folk. For a time things may seem to go on much as before, but the decisive power has entered in, and even mountains must move. *Prayer always creates a new situation.*

This is bare assertion, for no proof can be given save to faith, which finds in Christ assurance of a true revelation and a sure promise. It cannot be proved by instances, however numerous and wonderful. These all need the interpretation of faith. This, however, does not give assurance on a lower level than reason or a calculation of probabilities. It is the sole assurance we have or can have of every great spiritual truth or of any great moral value. And this interpretation by faith is absolute for him who believes in God.

This faith demands from us, if our habitual prayers are to be wholehearted, that we face honestly the disastrous elements in life, disastrous despite earnest and persistent prayer. We pray for peace and war comes. We seek healing for a friend and the disease increases. For another we pray for faith and the darkness thickens. We seek protection and the stroke falls.

> "O mother, praying God will save
> Your sailor: while your head is bow'd
> His heavy-shotted hammock-shroud
> Drops in his vast and wandering grave."
>
> TENNYSON—IN MEMORIAM.

If we ignore these we cut at the roots of our confidence in God, and steal from our intercessions their note of triumph and strength. It is not the purpose of this book to deal with questions of this kind, and seek to provide an answer for the many and difficult questions connected with prayer. Whether we think of them as conditioned by the absolute Will or the permissive Will or the thwarted Will of God, we have to recognize the

event *and learn to pray more deeply than the event.*
God takes to do with all these things, the God of
Love. They are not outside the action of that
love, whatever evil power has shaped the Cross
that marks them. God acts within them. Our
deeper intercession pleads with God there. In the
midst of the persisting evil the prayer is not " unanswered " in the purpose of His Will.

In our petitions and intercessions, perhaps
through disappointment about response, we have
sometimes to face an emotion, or absence of
emotion, which makes prayer difficult. Desire
and the sense of need are absent, and sullen
insensibility or vagrant worldliness invade the
mind. At such seasons few read books about
prayer, but danger lies by the roadside for many
who do, so I venture on three sentences of guidance. The supreme need, of course, is a penitent
return to God, and a reconversion of life such as
He alone can give. On the way to that it is good
to hold on to every scrap of worshipping custom
which remains possible, to " say a prayer " where
we once prayed, even if it be only the child's form
which once had meaning, to hold to the outer
observance though the inner life has gone, to do
the bare duty of homage though love for God and
life and good seems dead. We can resolve on this
and plan for it when there is life in our will and

our prayers, and hold to it in the day of defeat. Christ is not only life for the living but resurrection for the dead, and He comes into this valley of death.

There is an area of need which seems to lie wholly outside prayer. We cannot ask God to grant wrong desires which enter our hearts and exceed our needs in their violent demands or their sullen lurking persistency. Expressed to God, evil and even conquering as these are, they make a connection, not a barrier, between God and us. We can only shut God out by silence. "He knoweth our frame", as the wise Psalmist wrote, and we may come to God with surging passion in our heart, saying, "This is how I feel and what I want," and wait before Him knowing that He will not turn us away and that He will sympathize and help. Sympathize with evil? No, but sympathize with the human life at which it beats, with the temptation and the longing and the failure.

Men have, of course, sought to make God an accomplice in their sin. That is still a possibility. I do not fear that. I fear to shut out any part of life's longing or need or sin from openness with God. God takes action towards us as we come, and in the conflict of desires within us, sways life towards Himself. Christ " eateth and drinketh with publicans and sinners " not in some romantic gesture, but in life's daily sordidness and shame. We do not come to Him as those who, having put away evil, come to Him for pardon. We come to be delivered. If there be in us desire, half desire, stained desire, childish or frightened or evil desire, along with this approach in prayer, there is a pulse kept beating between God and the soul. God in His great skill and mercy uses even such an avenue as that for the influences of His Spirit. Christ uses even a bare and muddy road for His seeking and finding of the soul. The answer may be rebuke or some leading into a truer way, but God is not silent. "The only final failure of prayer is when man ceases to pray." Until then there is life passing between God and man, streaming in freedom from God or oozing in slow and sullen drops from man. There is some recognition of God even if it mistakes and distorts almost every feature of His Divine Being.

God is Shepherd of those who so halt on the way.

CHAPTER VIII

PENITENCE AND CONFESSION

" My own return to God in repentance is the greatest good I can do to any one else."
—Congreve's *Spiritual Order*, p. 66.

" So I saw in my Dream, that just as Christian came up with the Cross, his burden loosed from off his shoulders, and fell from off his back, and began to tumble; and so continued to do, till it came to the mouth of the Sepulchre, where it fell in, and I saw it no more.

" Then was Christian glad and lightsome, and said with a merry heart, He hath given me rest, by his sorrow; and life, by his death. Then he stood still a while, to look and wonder; for it was very surprising to him, that the sight of the Cross should thus ease him of his burden. . . . Then Christian gave three leaps for joy, and went on singing."
—Bunyan's *Pilgrim's Progress*.

THE general principles dealt with in this chapter are embodied in five main steps in the confession of sin.

Confession is made first to ourselves, following on knowledge of our sin in immediate recognition, or after honest search. Confession is then made to God, who alone can forgive and cleanse. This is

95

followed by acceptance of God's absolving and restoring grace. In the strength of that grace renunciation of sin is made. The spirit and mind are held open to any guidance from God towards undoing of evil and its results.

Associated with these are acknowledgment of our implication in the sin of the world: and of the need for cleansing from the soil of a day's mere living.

Confess. To whom? To God first? No. By God's help, confession to oneself. There is no real confession to God without that. We cannot confess to God what we only half acknowledge to ourselves. We are "standing on honesty" when we confess the sin we recognize. No other confession is genuine. However far we have departed from accepted standards of right conduct or feeling, unless we believe we have done wrong we cannot confess that we have, though we may well plead with God to guard us from self-deceit.

> "Search me, O God, and know my heart.
> Try me and know my thoughts.
> And see if there be any way of wickedness in
> me and lead me in the way everlasting."
> —PSALM CXXXIX.

This is likely to be a true prayer on the lips of one who is honest enough not to make conventional confessions to God.   And penitence goes far beyond specific confession.

The acknowledgment should be proportionate to the occasion.

To be merciless with anyone, even ourselves, is no virtue.   If there be no great sense of shame it is probably best not to try to stir it up, lest we create a kind of sentimental penitence.   When we try to be honest and to call things by their right names and to look at them fairly, we shall not be left unashamed.   To miscall things on either side, drawing a veil of exaggeration or a veil of excuse over this part of living is a common error.   We may regard ourselves as too busy to have time for prayer, when aversion to its demands is the real hindrance.   We may call ourselves sensitive, with a certain satisfaction that we are not clods, when it is jealousy that is wrong.   We may consider ourselves "highly strung", and be simply bad-tempered and unreasonable.   On the other hand scrupulosity is a very evil thing.   It is one of the devil's devices for withdrawing us from the battle with real sins to preoccupation with ourselves over trifles, a most unhealthy occupation, which hinders real warfare and real work.   Christ's spirit is given to enable us to live a normal healthy life, not to make us specialists in pathology, either of our own or of other people's moral diseases. Keen young folk and people with much leisure are specially prone to this exaggeration. And people busy about church work, strangely enough, need special warning. It is as easy a habit to acquire as is that of exaggerating other people's misdeeds—and that is easy enough.

Confession involves thought and openness to the voice of conscience. Without drawing out every detail, we admit to ourselves not only the presence of a tendency to evil, or of the real existence of evil, but of the evil as it manifests itself in incident. " I have done those things I ought not to have done, and have left undone those things I ought to have done." We may feel this truly and generally without confessing to ourselves *what* we have actually so done, and *what* left undone. There is a general and shamed feeling that yet never quite gets to grips with reality. It does not say " here, and to that person, and then, and in that way I did this thing that I ought not to have done ". The result of this is threefold: it hinders a true and full confession to God: it hinders the determined setting out to do what had been left undone: it shuts the door on the realization of full absolution. There is a world of difference between " I have not been true in speech ", and " On Friday I exaggerated the story I told about

A.B. so as to discredit him". When we make admissions like that to ourselves, then and not till then can we make a real confession to God; and the way is then open for God to tell us what to say or do.

Yes, but that is where the sting comes. We may not want to do anything more about it, may want it just to be passed over as forgiven and allowed to slip into the background. That is quite easy, so long as one acknowledges the general sin, but does not acknowledge the definite instance of Friday. It is so easy that it becomes equally easy to fall into the same sin on Saturday, and give it at last a habitual grip on life.

Our next action is confession to God. We can assume that any narration of the evil we have done is repeating to God what He knows already. When we have faced it and acknowledged it, it may be better for all, it certainly is better for some, not to repeat the details one has become conscious of, but to speak our confession to God in general terms. The thought which precedes the prayer is not detached from it and its contents are all in the prayer. Do not repeat them. Particularly does this seem wise when emotional centres have been concerned and anger or envy or jealousy or sex feelings or difficulty in forgiving injuries are involved. There are sins which we dare not recall in any detail. We cast them at the feet of God with shame and turn away our eyes. Unless our penitence is very complete and our will very resolute, the repetition of those evils in detail even to God is apt to bring a reliving of the occasion and the emotion. In the colder thought which precedes the prayer, and when we are judges of our own selves, this is not so apt to occur.

Having made our confession, as honestly as we can, and sought for pardon, we then open our hearts, a great act of faith, to a message of absolution. This is one of the most difficult and certainly one of the most Christian acts of faith, Christian in its view of God and in its trust in Him. "He pardoneth and absolveth all them that truly repent and unfeignedly believe His Holy Gospel." Often we bring our sin and the shame of it to Him, and we come away still burdened and depressed. There is something sorely lacking there, and yet we often feel as if to keep the burden were the only decent thing to do. We do not deserve to be released, and find it difficult to realize that our "deserving" has no share in this. It is all God's love.

So absolution and deliverance follow on penitent confession. These are God's part wholly, but we are not left in doubt about His action. Prophets and apostles and our Lord Himself have declared the sureness of this action of God towards penitent souls. There is nothing more sure than this promise. The imagery in which psalmists and prophets express it could not be more absolute. " As far as the East is from the West, so far hath He removed our transgressions from us." "Thou hast cast my sins behind Thy back." "Though thy sins be as scarlet, they shall be as white as snow." We come in faith. Let us go away in the same faith. I cannot think that God means a penitent soul to have anything less than a deep sense of deliverance.

At this point in prayer I have counselled the young folk in my care to stand up in acceptance of a real gift of God's grace. This symbolic action helps to convey the sense of an actual transaction taking place, and the need of deepening that sense does not belong only to youth. An old man bears glad testimony that such symbols are helpful to age also.

Confession to oneself and then confession to God with all our sin included, however few the words we use, and acceptance of His absolving grace. What comes next?

God is likely to have something to say to us about it all. Part of that will have been spoken to us in our self-acknowledgment. Restoration will be in our mind, if that be a thing possible. We do not need a special voice of God to make that known. Undoing, if anything can be undone; that also is in our common knowledge of God's will. The ordinary precautions against a repetition of the wrong will also be evident to our thought. The teaching of Christ, familiar in the Gospels, is always ready to our hand. The words and the spirit of the Lord Jesus are practical guidance, and we walk by them without needing to wait for special guidance, which would just repeat a familiar word. Yes, and yet God is likely to have a special word to speak, some recall of this common knowledge, some emphasis relevant to this individual confession, some avenue of restoration or undoing opened, beyond what we had thought of, some quickening of our sensitiveness and faculties, or some quite unlooked-for direction.

Confession to a wronged person is not to be ruled by any general principle. It will sometimes be absolutely necessary, yet there are many instances in life when making such confession inflicts a deeper injury and does a deadlier wrong. God's guidance is necessary in the intimate relationship between two human souls, wherever universal rules can be applied. Of course, the simplest way is to have a rule of confession, frank and complete. This gives relief to our own conscience, but equally it may give relief to our own vanity and self-esteem. It is a wounding and humbling thing to be thought to be trustworthy, and kind and good, when we know that here and there we have been false, and that our hidden life has been wrong. We may have to bear that and the shame of it in silence, where our confession would injure and wound. It is true, at the same time, that the only way may be confession, however much that wounds another, and the injury we then inflict is the most bitter fruit of our sin. The whole realm is full of sensitive chords, faith and courage and cowardice and selfishness. We need guidance, not by a general prescription, but by the spirit of God in each separate case.

At some point in these prayers of penitence there should be a definite act of will, in which we with honesty and strength of purpose renounce our sin. It is possible that even such a thing as confession of sin may become one of the indulgences of life and have little effect on conduct. We may confess and seek pardon from God and keep a door open towards our sin. That is not enough for real contrition. There is cause to fear a long succession of broken promises or vows, but more cause to fear the confession which does not involve a sincere purpose, and does not expect any fullness of answer to the cry for help which is at the heart of real confession. Where expectancy of deliverance is lost, penitence loses its spring of life, for we then feel ourselves in the grip of a necessity which rules our life. "Making no provision for the flesh to obey the lust thereof," is the guidance of St. Paul. In that spirit *we renounce as well as confess* our sin.

This comes most fitly after we have heard God's absolving message. The way for our feet which God shows as He gives His pardoning grace is such as we could not walk without the new life and strength this grace gives.

There is another area into which our penitence should enter, the sin of the world. It is no sentimental theory which asserts that all men have responsibility towards the common sin of humankind. *The world's sin is our own sin.* We cannot passively acquiesce or treat it as inevitable. We share responsibility for it, and when we face that till it wounds and pains, then we are taking our proper place in the brotherhood of mankind. The misery and weariness of the world's sin become part of our own pain, so that the heart is filled with pity and with purpose to seek that saving grace be brought into contact with the sin of the world. Here, too, hopefulness and expectation are born. The sin of others is united with our penitence and with our experience of the loving-kindness and the

saving mercies of Christ. We bring men penitence
by repenting. We learn to hope for the world,
because we have found boundless mercy towards
ourselves and cannot despair for others. So
penitence is bound up with intercession as with
thanksgiving.

As we look back on the day's life we sometimes
find that nothing stands out as an act or deed of
sin. We are being quite open with ourselves and
with God, and we look for His revealing light—
and nothing stands out. There are eager souls who
then begin to hunt for sins, feeling sure that they
must have sinned somewhere, and end by manu-
facturing sins, turning innocent mistakes into the
resemblance of deliberate wilfulness, and absorption in the day's work into neglect of God. Here
is a better way. Very humbly and *gratefully we
accept that day from God*, and ask Him to cleanse
us from the stain of the day's living, and from
"hidden faults". The great prayer in the nine-
teenth psalm runs:

" Who can discern his errors?
   Clear Thou me from hidden faults.
   Keep back Thy servant also from presumptuous sins."

That prayer exactly fits us. As we deal honestly
with the sins that lift up their heads, God will give
us discernment about the hidden faults, and we

G

can praise Him who has kept us through such a blessed day.

This recalls another need. At the end of a common day's life, with all care, and no deliberate handling of unclean things, our hands are soiled. Life in this world is like that. Even our bodies, clothed and covered from contact with the outside world, are soiled. Living in the world we know inevitably brings defiling. So is it with soul and spirit. The day's living, in contact with much that is stained with evil, in the common world we know, brings its own soiling and weakening. At the close of the day, even where no deliberate sin appears, we ask for cleansing from the dust of the way, the soil of the day's life with all its contacts. And God gives it, with refreshing and renewal and rest in His gift. Truly we need this. It is no shame to a man to come from his day's work with soiled hands. They have been soiled in the inevitable contact with soiling things, and are more honourable in their stain than hands that have kept their whiteness by withdrawal from the world's life. Yet they are soiled and unclean. It is shame to him if he leaves them so, and eats and sleeps without the washing he should give. Then he becomes truly a dirty person. This is true of the spiritual life also. It is no disgrace that the soiling of the day's life affects our souls; it is disgrace if we suffer it to remain uncleansed and accept the defilement. So we ask God for cleansing from " the dust of the way ". How willingly Christ washed His disciples' feet!

CHAPTER IX

DRUDGERY AND DISCIPLINE

> " The nature that is endued with the capacity for prayer, the soul that can be filled with the disclosure of His Goodness, the life that was meant to find its highest exercise, its point of illumination, its way to rise, in seeking Him, cannot without hurt refuse all this. Prayer is, for spiritual beings, a law of health—a law which we may put back and ignore persistently in this life if we will, but which we cannot change."
>
> —PAGET, *The Spirit of Discipline*, 288.

The Drudgery of Prayer

THE great Augsburg Confession speaks of the " faith which is not the mere knowledge of an historical fact, but that which believes not only the history but the effect of that history upon the mind ". That wise sentence encourages us not to look upon the act of prayer alone, but upon its inevitable and usual connections. One of these is, or at least wears the uniform of, Drudgery, the toilsome plodding with heavy step on an accustomed way. Prayer drudgery! Never! "Now stand we on the top of happy hours!" Good—but the way to that for many believing souls becomes at times full of oppositions and restraints, obstacles and ambushes. We come to prayer at times (often?) against our inclination and the upper stratum of our will. Sustained by our deeper will, and a divine gift too little recognized, we force ourselves to take the way of prayer. The impelling force is really the hand of God. "Sit down doggedly to it, sir," was the advice given by a wise professor to a student who found it difficult to write sermons. It is good advice about prayer when the "shades of the prison house" close in on us. Kneel down doggedly—how far it seems from the "sweet hour of prayer" experience, which also is true. We face and carry through as a task what in our hearts we know to be our highest privilege. That is drudgery. Blessed be drudgery: it means that we are not yielding to the foes of the spirit; that we are prevailing against our own earth-bound nature; that we are breaking through our inertia and worldliness; that we are conquering. If we cease praying, we are beaten men. Blessed be drudgery: it is a real way to God. What else could we expect in bringing a nature like ours to so high and spiritual and sensitive an enterprise as communion with God.

" Myrrh at His Cross's foot I lay—
  All my dull worth of patience harshly strong
  To plod by day and night my short life long
  (Grim on God's errands gay)
  His own parched foot-sore way."

What A. S. Cripps thus writes of the work he loves with all his heart is true of prayer, as of all Christian enterprise.

Keeping in mind the drudgery as well as the joy of prayer, the deep triumphant joy of it, and the refreshing and the rest, I set down some of its connections.

Learning to pray is for many a real task, which calls for thought, endurance, imagination, and strength of will. Beginning anew after a time of neglect is also a difficult thing, when the first restoring impulse has died away. In the helpful sermon on " Sin and Law " quoted at the head of this chapter, Bishop Paget writes: " The desire to pray may disappear, just as for a lazy man there may cease to be any pleasure in the healthy use of his limbs. Like him, we may find it hard distasteful work at first to take up again what we have long abandoned. But if we yield to that distaste, if we acquiesce in our inertness, we are withholding the effort which an essential law of our life demands from us." It is wise to recognize these facts, for they are facts in the life of so many. We recognize then also the need of special help from God and seek it from Him. We recognize the need of bringing our whole power of resolution and will to the task before us. It is not a light enterprise in which we engage. Power of resolution and will may enable us to adopt methods of prayer and hold to them doggedly, to set aside times and observe them in the face of all difficulties. That is only building a framework for prayer, but there also we are sustained by the essential thing, the supernatural gift, the never-failing presence of God, responding to our need. The very building, the laying of these bricks, is the voice of our deep desire, and is prayer in deepest reality. In another figure we may think of our task as preparing the way for communion with God. It is seeking to obey the prophetic word, "Prepare ye the way of the Lord, make His paths straight." This way is made crooked and rough by default of our own natures, by our habits, by our circumstances, by the sin of the world and by our own. All these hinder our communion, and so far this "way of the Lord" is not straight or level. Yet it is open, and we keep on the road of prayer, even if all the traveller's joy be gone, plodding on in the dark. When we cease to pray *that* way is blocked, whatever other ways are open. We meet at this place, as in all life, the constant relationship and paradox of man's effort and God's full and unmerited gift. Grace is always a bestowal, communion with God is a bestowal, and our plodding preparations hold the prophetic assurance "Every valley shall be exalted, and every mountain and hill shall be made low, and the crooked shall be made straight and the rough places plain, and the glory of the Lord shall be revealed." So we plod on and trust!

There are disciplines and customs which help us towards this faithfulness. It is a matter of common knowledge that all our faculties can be purified in intention, strengthened in purpose, and made more effective by recognized practices and disciplines. Memory can be strengthened and its contents made more available by suitable means. Will-power can be increased. The emotional nature can be controlled and regulated by appropriate training. The intellectual faculties are not fixed, and their quality is affected by our reading and our thinking, by the areas in which we exercise them, and the food for thought which we supply.

It is a fair deduction that prayers, *in which all these faculties are involved*, are affected in their range, their depth and their insight, their purpose and truth, by just these same disciplines. Much of this, most of this indeed, will be unconscious, but the recognition of the fact is vitally important. We are the same people when we

pray as we are at other times, and no one need
expect his praying to possess qualities of earnestness, concentration of purpose, vision, joy of communion with God, when his life is habitually
lacking in these things. Our praying is an expression of our living, just as our living is the expression of our praying. When we are seeking to
make progress in prayer it is an encouragement
to remember that as we learn to pray more faithfully we inevitably are learning to live more
faithfully.

The word "disciplines" is deliberately used as
meaning the ordered control of outward action
and inward mood in accordance with Christian
common sense, the common sense of disciples of
Jesus, whose lives hold a controlling purpose and
are travelling towards a goal. There is liberty for
a child without this discipline of life, there is no
such liberty for a grown person who would share
the life of Christ. There is a way of freedom,
real freedom with a sense of leisure and sufficiency
of time and strength, with room for a measure of
puckishness, with room to take advantage of the
unexpected event in life, and the casual opportunity. It is open only to those who live a disciplined life. Using an analogy from another
sphere: it is those who order the spending of their
money in a disciplined way, learning what it is

essential to provide for, what must be refused and what restrained, who also have sufficiency for casual needs, freedom from the strain of debt and from the burden of disorderly finances.

A useful comparison can be made between our learning to pray and our learning to do anything else. We wish, for instance, to learn some foreign language. We may be able to set aside only five minutes a day for that, or may give five hours, but in each case the procedure is the same. We give up something, even if it be only idle dreaming, that this may come in. We appoint a set time. We decide on a normal line of procedure within that time, usually determined by the book of instruction. There is (according to our varying ideas about the value of this new language) the use of opportunities during the day for revision or application. The shorter the time available, the more carefully it must be arranged and the more exactly kept, but the same principles apply as in the longer time. Obviously the man who so sets aside an appointed time and knows the path he is going to take through it, is likely to arrive at a fair mastery of the language more swiftly and thoroughly, than he who resolves to "find some time" during the day, and who uses that time in less orderly ways.

So is it with prayer. It is very wise to appoint

times, fixed appointments, only to be set aside in some urgent necessity. If this can only be five minutes, or an hour or more, is not of first importance. What does matter is that it should be a time proportionate to the worth of its purpose and to the circumstances of the individual. It is wise, whether the time be long or short, to have a careful plan for its use. Special interests or needs may change the plan and the time be more wisely used in a different way, but it is good to have a normal plan so that no time is lost in deciding what to do next. Again, as with the language lesson, it is wise that this interest on which our heart is set in the separated time, should not be left behind when that time is over. The day will bring opportunities and calls in which there is application of these separated prayers and resolves.

Another detail in the comparison is worth noting. The language student who has five hours for his study and his practice may be able to spare time to rearrange things every day. The student with five minutes for his use cannot do that, and must come with a prearranged plan—even for prayer.

CHAPTER X

THIS chapter is more the personal testimony of a Scottish Presbyterian than a general reflection on the value and use of books of prayer.

The use or non-use of the recognized Prayer and Service Books is largely affected by training and temperament and ecclesiastical tradition—and by prejudice. I find the use of them helpful, especially when it appears wise to change from the more strenuous ways of prayer, when very tired, or in illness, or the even more trying days of convalescence. They widen the area of prayer, teaching of things dear to the heart of God which had no part in my prayers, reminding me of blessings which were ignored in my thanksgiving. This benefit has been more pronounced when the books read were those of other denominations than my own, and so were less familiar.

I find them often helpful in giving the word or

phrase which gathers up most fitly what is in my heart and deepens its meaning. The power of the right word in purifying and strengthening prayer is very great.

This help is, in reality, not the reading of a book, but the grace of God in other men called to our room to open our eyes, to increase the width and intensity of our vision, and the range of our sympathy. We know the blessing on "the two or three" in united prayer. We may gather the two or three beside us as we sit alone and enter into the prayers which they enable us to appropriate by the printed form.

What are other men praying about?—for whom?—and how do they pray? Our lives and our prayers are enriched when we have this knowledge and pray with them. Especially is this true in the use of the great scriptural prayers, of the Church of England Prayer Book with its inimitable prayers and collects, and of the great hymns in common use.

The worth of these deepens when *read aloud*, and when there gathers round them the thought of those who in the past have prayed thus, of the occasions on which they have been sung or said, the words become living words, sanctified by their use. Their private use deepens their value in public worship.

Among the lesser books, it may be wise to choose one rather than to read over a number. The one is used deeply and explored with care. After it has yielded up its treasures, and these are added to the coin of regular use, another mine can be opened.

In all books of prayer, selection and re-translation is needed, and it is quite likely that their noble and classical language does not appeal to a number of more modern folk. The emotional background and the theological formulas of Wesley or Newton, of Keble or Newman, of David and Asaph and the Sons of Korah, may detract from their value for some. One can re-translate. The substance and the vision and the devotion are all there, and can be expressed in our own tongue, and set against our own background.

Another range of vision and prayer-impulse is to be found in books which do not set out to be devotional, but which do reveal God to man— books of biography, song, poetry, story, not professedly religious. Personal testimony is very limited, but many more than I find in such sources as these compulsions to prayer and service as strong and deep as in professedly devotional books.

In gradually building up a prayer book of their

own, collecting prayers from other books or composing for themselves a number of people find
great gain.   It has its own dangers, especially for
those with literary gifts.   The turn of a phrase
may become of more importance than the truth
it seeks to express; the form displace the reality
of devotion.   More readily, however, in this realm
of life beauty of form, so long as it is simple,
deepens the reality of devotion and wings it with
earnestness.   Whatever theory of Inspiration we
hold with regard to the Holy Scriptures, it is
universal belief that their exquisite beauty of
form is part of the power which is exercised over
us by the great voices of faith and love.   The
51st Psalm, for instance, an intensely personal
prayer, is " composed " with supreme artistry, and
any sinful man may use it in confession.   The
acrostic Psalms are compositions developing to
great elaboration in such as Psalm 119.   (In its
Hebrew form, the first group of eight verses has
each verse beginning with the first letter of the
Hebrew alphabet.   The second group begins each
verse with the second letter, and so on through
the twenty-two groups.)   The thirty-fifth chapter
of Isaiah would not move our souls with the same
hope and trust were its music not so exquisite.
With these before us we need not fear to use our
pens, or to reap help from the work of others,

in expressing our prayers to God, though the elaborate forms are unsafe as models for us. Part of our religious heritage in " Disruption " Scotland is a common belief that the work of the Holy Spirit is limited to improvisation, that when a pen or a book is used prayer becomes " man-made " and dead. In the spiritual glow of evangelical revival, men have often lost sight of the fact that the Spirit normally works through the reason and imagination and will and purpose of men, and that these are stimulated, not restricted, by reading and writing and thought. In the North we are still somewhat embarrassed by this heritage, a precious thing for another day and circumstance, and so many read-prayers and written-prayers, even more sung-prayers, have a fainter glow of the Spirit's desire in them. There is a real sense of values in this, and historically it rose from a purifying and strengthening belief in the inspiration of God, clothing man's desire with fit utterance, and carrying him beyond the bounds of his own vision or thought. It is disastrous when such a faith dies away, in a congregation or an individual. The deductions that have been drawn from it have often been mistaken, and it is that part of the heritage which still hinders the liberty of many. Careful, studied expressions of our need and our love are as open to the influence of the Spirit as an unpremeditated prayer. That influence pours forth on us from other men's prayers, when these are true.

The value of the prayer lies in its use, not its composition, its power to bring man into communion with God. God's response is the essential element, not our way of expression. Whatever way of prayer brings that response is the right way for a man to take.

Such a book of prayers, and of single sentences of prayer grows in value. It has clinging memories —perhaps regrets which purify, perhaps joys which relive, perhaps desires which quicken again in the heart. It will certainly be a revealing thing as one considers it in other days and sees how the knowledge of God grows, and the emphasis of prayer varies. Yes, make a prayer book for yourself, if you are in the way of writing.

Another less usual prayer book for swift night prayers is a map of the world. Heavy black lines run from Britain and divide the world into six fairly equal parts. To each a certain night is assigned. Thus on Monday the eye passes across the North Sea with its great fishing fleets, and up to the pole, over North Europe and Russia, China and Japan. Storm and harsh labour and fishermen, the Arctic peoples and fleets, Russia and its infinite variety of peoples, its government, exiles,

churches, propaganda, enthusiasms, and atheisms.
Then China with its sorrows, wars, burdens, persecutions, saints, churches, missions; and Japan,
action and spirit, war and desire, need and passion,
religion and people.   In viewing all this the heart
is at prayer, rarely with specific request, but *in a
quiet movement of blessing, and desire of salvation for it all*.   It is journeying in the love of God,
connecting His desire with some vision of the
teeming life.   A minute can suffice for such a
passing from land to land, with swift thought of
the whole or of any appealing part, *and a blessing
on it*.   A minute can be spent in peopling land
and sea with figures whose life or circumstances
we dimly know.   The scene changes with each
new view.   It is extraordinary how much even one
single minute can contain and how much the heart
can give.

So each night we gather swiftly into the heart
a vision of one great part of the world, till in
the six nights we have passed over all the world.
As part of this, we say the Lord's Prayer with
special desire that each clause be fulfilled in the
life of that needy world.   The more removed it
is from the hallowing of God's name or the life
of His Kingdom or the doing of His Will, the
more urgent will our prayer be.   The more our
own hearts live in the compassion of Jesus Christ,

the more truly will we seek for this world daily bread, forgiveness, deliverance from evil. We stand inside the world of the vision with all its infinite variety of life, and taking its need on our hearts say "*Our* Father". There is no need of the world which is not covered by these six petitions.

In ourselves, such a journeying of prayer works change. We read the news of social movements, political issues, international diplomacies, economic movements, and find them lifted into a new realm, the realm of God's love and care. The Light of that great prayer falls on them, and their issues, in turn, beat at it. They are changed for us. We judge all things "In the love of Christ".

Our nightly journeying has in it also special points. The face of a friend appears. Some deeper interest marks a place, a phase of life or death. There are revelations from the Unknown, and from the Known, as it opens its life more fully. There is no end to the freshness of view.

I venture to commend some such practice for a month of trial, with a very short time given to it nightly, perhaps two minutes. If it grips you so that you want longer time, I should suggest that ordinarily you do not allot to it more than five minutes. Occasionally you may survey the world for as long as you choose, but that is better done at another time. In any practice which uses the imagination as this does, there is a tendency to lose the sense of reality and pass from praying to dreaming. The latter is good, now and then. It helps to people the world of our thoughts with real men and women. Our purpose nightly, however, is to gather the world into our prayers. In the few minutes there is time for keen and changing vision, but dreaming is excluded. For the same reason I recommend that prayer here be normally a benediction and the Lord's Prayer. These will both grow in the fullness of their desire, but it is good to keep to the all-including words.

Should it be that God calls you to fuller use of this way of prayer, of course you will obey. I write only of " beginnings ".

(My own map cost 1d. It has the meridian line down the centre and the dividing lines are drawn from Britain. The two lines to the east reach, one to the Equator, and the other to a point 60 degrees south latitude; the centre line passes with a little adjustment through Britain and the North and South Poles; the lines to the west reach, one to the Equator, and the other to 60 degrees south latitude. The chief continents and larger islands fall almost completely into one or other of these divisions, although one division contains a portion of both Americas.   This is not meant to be a scientific division!)

CHAPTER XI

FOR BUSY PEOPLE

LIFE which is overtired and has no leisure and quietness in prayer is unnatural, however common it may be. Often that condition is due to misjudgment of life's purpose and values, to the choice of the temporal rather than the eternal. Often it is due to mistaken theories of faithfulness in God's service, which ignore His own guidance and command. This is very common with ministers, missionaries and students. Often it is due to sheer driving necessity. This bears on women more than on men, and very specially on mothers with young children.

It is not the task of this book to discuss these causes. It assumes that in every case the overbusy life is unavoidable. So its task is to suggest practices which may keep alive the flame of prayer in these difficult circumstances. If habits of prayer be laid aside in the burdened days, the days of more leisure may find them difficult to resume. More vital still is the need to preserve unhurried communion with God in the present days just because they are so distracting and busy.

The practices commended, few out of a great number, have all been found helpful in actual experience, some at one time, some at another. They are not a sequence. They are not only for overworked people, but have values for those with leisure.

May I ask you to associate with this, Chapters I and XII, and page 121ff., which speak of the same subject.

Note that the word "unhurried" applies to a short interval, say five minutes, as really as to an hour or two. This depends on the freedom of spirit within the assigned period, not on its duration, and this freedom of spirit, not under bondage to "the next thing", depends in the first place on the limitation which we set on ourselves and the arrangements we make to use the time most suitably. We begin, knowing that we have plenty of time for what we mean to do, and we do not try to crowd into a few minutes what can only be done with an hour at our disposal.

Prayer during Work

There can be no doubt that a number of people, specially hardworking women, can think and pray with least distraction when their hands are em-

ployed. They rarely sit down with folded hands
to think. The sense of many things waiting to
be done hinders freedom of thought. Let the
fisher's wife take up her knitting, however, and
her thoughts are free. So is it with the housewife
at any semi-mechanical part of her work, such as
dusting or washing of dishes or clothes.

It is a definite gain that for such a time
which regularly recurs, and for equivalent times
in a man's life, a certain devotional exercise be
arranged. In Chapter II it is suggested that each
day a set number of causes for thanksgiving be
specially realized and noted. The same can be
done with some, say three, of the worthy desires
of life. This would seem to be one suitable time
for their choosing and realization. At some time
in the busy life, when the hands are engaged in
some mechanical task, three definite causes of
satisfaction are called to mind and three active
desires. These are connected with the thought of
God and of God's care. One may say in the
simplest words "Thank you" to God, or make a
rather fuller acknowledgment: "I am very glad
about these things"; "You have been very good
to me about these things." So also with the requests: "I ask that these things may come to
me." Kneeling or standing makes no difference,
and at least this much of prayer is everywhere

possible, and possible to most types of mind.

It is not likely that thought about these things will end with the mere naming of them; and the regular choosing of these, with a certain measure of thought upon them, passes over into very heart-felt communion with God.

Of course, I do not advocate an attempt to fill all such occasions in this way, but the use of one such opportunity is of value, as is the recognition that direct communion with God is possible while the hands and the automatic function of the brain are engaged. Even for people with plenty of leisure there is value in this, for it helps to bring control and recognition of God into testing and formative areas of life which are not always recog-nized as testing or formative, the areas of spon-taneous, instinctive, undirected thinking.

Swift Morning Prayer

Whatever time be set apart for longer devotions, it is of vital importance that the first waking moments of each day be directed towards God. Instantly, with the return of thought and aware-ness after sleep, the good and evil influences which affect life become operative in a specially forceful way. Many a day is made or marred by these first moments and by the response we make then to the calls of life. It is wise therefore to prepare a way by which the first thoughts and first responses are turned Godwards. Till this is natural, habitual, and inevitable, we need to make it deliberate and planned. Something has to be shut out—the door closed. Something has to be deliberately sought and practised. The laws by which habits mental and spiritual are formed and confirmed operate here as they do everywhere, and the deliberately chosen way becomes in time the unconscious and natural path. At first, and later in passing through special experiences, we may have to fight hard to hold possession of these first moments for the Godward look and response. Worries, plans, temptations, interests of many kinds strive for possession, and what they get they often hold and their influence colours all the day. If God be first in our choice, the day will be coloured and affected by that choice through all its hours. So we do well to set before ourselves as a definite purpose, that our first waking life be turned towards God.

Here is a practice for which time and privacy can be secured in the busiest day, and which yet affects vitally the whole of life.

Begin the day by offering it and yourself to God. Look at the day as an individual thing that begins and ends with completeness in itself; then take this thing, this day, and offer it to God to be a day for His use. I would suggest that you write down a short form of such dedication, something after this pattern: "Lord of my life and God of my salvation, I offer this day to Thee. I would seek in all things to do Thy will, and use its hours as Thou wilt guide." I suggest the use of some such form prepared by yourself, so that morning by morning you do not need to think of words in which to express yourself, but saying the familiar words *slowly and deliberately* you can send your will travelling along these familiar lines. If the form begins to lose meaning, change it, and you can add to it a sentence of petition for grace for yourself, and a sentence of intercession for those you love. Now this does not take long. Only a minute or two with some concentration of the will, and what is the effect? The day at once becomes a unity and the life becomes unified. However many distracting details come into the day, both mind and emotion are dominated, not by them but by the sense that you have only one thing to do—namely, to act in obedience to God with regard to them. The effect of that in preventing the nervous sense of over-pressure is very great indeed. You pass from one thing to another, not as one leaping from side to side, but as one marching steadily forward with a single object in life—to use the day for God. There is

a second great effect: that as you go out con-
sciously to a day *offered* to God, that becomes
God's opportunity to use you in fuller measure
than before. The ordinary routine of life may
go on outwardly without apparent change, but
the life meeting that routine finds that all things
are new.

Use a Creed

Begin the day by affirming your faith in God,
and thus seeking His grace for the day's need.
Whatever your creed be, not so much the thing
you believe in the way of some vague tradition,
but the thing which in your reasonable mind you
have accepted as truth for you—take your stand
on that as the day begins. A number of us would
express that in the words of the Apostles' Creed,
although with our own interpretation of some of
its clauses. Whether that or some other be the
adequate expression of your faith, renew it every
day and take your stand on it for the day's living.
Pull yourself erect, "stand to attention", and
with deliberation speak, whether with outward
expression or not, the words of your creed. Try
at the same time to throw that faith forward to
meet all that the day will bring. "I believe in
God the Father Almighty." Simply to take your
stand on that dispels a number of fears which

might otherwise haunt life all the day. "And in Jesus Christ His only Son our Lord": to affirm that changes misty glimpses of God to that which Christ clearly revealed, and recalls the sense of his Lordship over you and your day. So you take your stand on every clause of that which you believe, and you go out to meet the day with that declaration of a faith active and effective for life's need. Even the most vital of our beliefs get into the background of life and get clouded or altogether hidden by some prevailing need or temptation. It makes a real difference to life, and is a source of strength when we begin every day by making explicit to ourselves the presence and prevailing power of God and what we believe concerning Him. The person who does this regularly will find that opportunity comes each day for renewal of the dedication and the faith, and that both need and desire will reveal other opportunities of prayer, with wider vision and more full detail. It takes only a very few moments to do this deliberately, and the day finds you setting out as a *believer in God*.

At another time certainly, because it deals with faith on a different level, and not with quite so sure a rock beneath your feet, you may do well, also, to extend your creed into human relationships; for the joy and power of these also need to be made explicit. Your real faith in your friends and in the dear relationships of home life gets obscured at times by irritating ways which bulk out of true proportion and hinder the expression of love and trust, and end in sapping away some portion of its strength and joy. It is not a foolish exercise sometimes to continue your creed, and say not only "I believe in God", but "I believe in——" naming husband or wife or parent or friends or child. Indeed, one may go beyond this and say: "I believe in men despite all the evil of their ways, because I believe in Christ Jesus. I believe in that spark of God which is in the heart of everyone whom I shall meet this day." Then one meets men with a different expectation, sees in them what otherwise cannot be seen, and speaks to them with a deeper courtesy, reverencing God in them.

Lack of privacy. This is so often associated with lack of time that it may have a little place here. Great numbers have no opportunity of being alone in the ordinary course of the day.

To kneel down before others in the common family sitting-room or a shared lodging may be a testimony, but it does not make for detached and sincere prayer. The presence of people otherwise occupied is distracting, and if there is a feeling that they are not in perfect sympathy, it is

exceedingly difficult to settle the mind on the
prayers we would offer. It seems as if our Lord
Himself felt this, even with His disciples. He
"went out a long while before day"; He "removed a little way"; He "sent His disciples away
and went up to the mountain top alone"; He
advised His disciples when they prayed to go into
a private place and shut the door. It is almost
essential that this part of prayer must be in separation from others, so that their presence adds no
distraction.

On the other hand, it would seem quite needful
that our Bible reading should become recognized
in the family as a habit, normal and usual, as
reading a newspaper is. When that is so it
attracts no attention and there is not much distraction in receiving its message. In that reading,
prayer may become quite natural and undis-
tracted, because we know that the others in the
room are not criticizing. Our clasped hands, as
our thinking changes to praying, do not call the
attention of the others. Having thought of the
substance and intention of our prayers we may
leave the room for some private expression of
these, if that be felt needful. Again, it may be
possible for some to use for expressed prayer a
few minutes of the darkness after one is in bed,
or in the morning before rising, and in that we

are taking a way which the psalmists knew and which they praised. The planned and wise use of available intervals like these invariably opens the way for other opportunities and reveals unexpected places in life where prayer can find its expression. That these short intervals should be filled to the brim, it is probably wise to make preparation at a more leisurely time.

CHAPTER XII

CELLS OF PRAYER

This chapter is an attempt to describe, with "reasons annexed", a practice of the devotional life which a number of people have found useful. It is specially helpful for those who begin their day early, live it with little leisure and end it tired. It is helpful when emergencies, emergencies which tend to grow chronic, occur in our life and disturb the regular ways of private prayer. Travelling, illness in the home, an extra rush of work, an influx of guests and other causes disturb the usual order of things, and sometimes threaten to become the usual order of things. The morning prayers become hurried, and at night body and mind and spirit are very tired and prayer is difficult. Sometimes prayer in the usual forms stops altogether. It is that state of need which this special practice looks to.

To express it, the form of simple "Instruction" is chosen.

The suggestion is that certain forms of prayer should be chosen or composed by which the soul can make its approach to God and find a means of communion with Him. These forms of prayer cover a range of gratitude and desire appropriate to the occasion of their use, and they are chosen of sufficient length to occupy in their use *five minutes of leisurely unhurried prayer*. The purpose of this is to provide a short and yet comprehensive order of prayer which can be used when all the faculties are at their keenest and call forth the exercises of every faculty, and which yet can be used when every faculty is dulled by weariness or confused by many beckoning needs, and when without such help it would be difficult to engage in such comprehensive prayer.

An example is given here which assumes five minutes as a possible time. To use this to the full and still to possess the reality of quiet leisure the application of certain common-sense principles is necessary. The time must not be filled too full or the unhurried communion is lost. The prayers chosen for that time should be the deepest and most unchanging which lie in our hearts. The nature and the order of the prayers are prepared beforehand. The words of the prayers are prepared, written or held in memory, and are not

varied except at long intervals. Again it should
be emphasized that these should not be more
than can be used without *haste* in this little cell
of prayer which is occupied for five minutes and
which we ourselves have builded.

A sense of leisure is preserved by making sure
that what we are going to do can be deliberately,
even slowly, done within the time. The words
spoken must not exceed what can be said very
deliberately, with a little pause after each clause,
in five minutes. A sense of separation is acquired
by making such outward arrangements as prevent,
to the utmost limit possible, any interruption, and
by deliberately withdrawing into this " devotion ".
It does not belong to the clanging day. It is a
" cell " built off the highway. The sense of
seclusion within a cell becomes real and adds to
the sense of leisure. On the other hand, as there
is no need to " watch the time ", which is guarded
by the chosen wording of the prayers, the sense of
independence-of-time adds to the sense of separation.

Here is such a cell for the morning. Anyone
repeating these words slowly and earnestly with
a pause between each clause will find that they
occupy something between four and five minutes.
First there is an act of adoration, then a short
prayer uniting thanksgiving for the night's rest

and the committal of the day to God; following that comes a short prayer commending certain loved friends by name and others unnamed to God's care; following this there is an act of faith, an affirmation of the soul's trust in God; and lastly, the prayer which our Lord taught His disciples.

"*Now blessed be the God of Israel, who only doeth wondrous things. And blessed be His Glorious Name for ever: and let the whole earth be filled with His glory. Amen, and Amen.*"

(Psalm 72.)

"*Almighty God, my King and Saviour, I offer Thee my thanks for the night's rest and for all the hope of this new day, looking to Thee for Thy blessing on its work and its rest. I offer to Thee now my thoughts and my words, my actions and my resting, my temptations and any suffering that may come, that Thou mayest use them for any purpose of Thy Holy Will. I seek that this day be wholly Thine. By the Grace of Jesus Christ. Amen.*"

"*O God, the giver of all love, who hast given me the blessings of friendship, I thank Thee for all my friends. I commit into Thy loving care . . . all other friends unnamed, and those whom I shall meet in the course of this day. May the Grace of the Lord Jesus Christ, Thy love, O God, and the Communion of Thy Holy Spirit, be with them all. Amen."*

"I believe in God the Father Almighty, Maker of heaven and earth, and in Jesus Christ His only son, our Lord. . . . I believe in the Holy Ghost, the holy Catholic Church, the communion of saints, the forgiveness of sins, the resurrection of the body and the life everlasting. Amen."

"Our Father, which art in Heaven, hallowed be Thy name. Thy Kingdom come, Thy will be done, in earth as it is in heaven. Give us this day our daily bread. And forgive us our debts as we forgive our debtors. And lead us not into temptation, but deliver us from evil: For Thine is the kingdom, the power, and the glory, for ever. Amen."

If it becomes the habit of life to withdraw, as is surely always possible, for five minutes at set intervals of the day into such a cell of prayer, and reverently and slowly to speak these words to God with such meaning and desire as we can bring to their utterance, the result will be a strengthened and quietened life in the hours following. It is not suggested, nor would it be normally at all worthy, that such a five minutes' retirement should constitute anyone's normal way and time of communion with God in expressed prayer, but it is claimed that with such retirement made a part of longer devotions and then used when longer devotions are impossible, there is provided a valuable aid to faithfulness and reality in our communion with God. Prayer involves in its full exercises the faculties of thought and memory, emotion and will. When life is hurried, the haste affects them, so that there is not the same clearness or depth in their use. When one is tired, even although the weariness has not come to the point of sheer exhaustion, these faculties are affected and no one of them has its normal power. At such times it is a relief to be delivered from the necessity of choosing the way of prayer, or the words in which prayer is to be expressed. Here, prepared beforehand in thought and earnestness, there is a way along which the soul can travel and there are words which become dearer and more full of meaning as they are regularly used, because of the response of God to their use. They are not words chosen, and the direction of the prayer is not chosen, by Church or organization outside ourselves, they are chosen in accordance with our will and express our own heart's desire. Even if any of them are words of another's forming, as is the Lord's Prayer, *we choose them as our own.*

For the night-time a similar cell is prepared. It will contain just what the heart desires to put into it. Here is one such arrangement, out of an infinite variety:

An act of adoration: this is always the lighting of the lamp of prayer.

A prayer which looks back at the day in gratitude and in penitence.

A prayer for those we love.

The offering of the night hours to God even as the day hours were offered: sleep, memories, thoughts, desires, dreams, the awaking.

An expression of faith, in a shorter form than in the morning (Rom. viii. 38-9 is very suitable).

The Lord's Prayer in its special use as intercession, the " our " used in its widest comprehension.

Some may wish to prepare a cell for the middle of the day. Here again is an example:

An act of adoration (so much depends on this, especially at the time when the pressure of the world is greatest).

An act of recall of life's purpose. (Such, for instance, as the two great commandments: "Thou shalt love the Lord thy God, with all thy heart and with all thy soul and with all thy strength and with all thy mind; and thy neighbour as thyself.")

A prayer for the vision of God in the busy ways.

Or, instead of the above sequence, we may use only a quiet recital of the *Te Deum*. This has a wide range of prayer, and in using it one is united with "all the saints" of Christian faith.

Going back to the details of the first example: it is surely wise in such a brief opportunity of communion to begin with an act of adoration which sets God before us in His infinite glory. The thanksgiving and the committal of the day to God have also adoration in them, and desire for his glory. So many of the experiences of life seem useless, especially do some of our sufferings seem useless and only weakening and restricting, as do our temptations. Much of the daily occupation of many of us in shop or office or factory, much of the work of the home, seems as if it were of little

use to the world, or for the Kingdom of God.
When all life is offered to God the whole thing
changes. If it be such work as we have any right at
all to do, even the right of earning our daily bread,
then God can use it. The thing in which we can
see no good or purpose, suffering or temptation,
given over to Him, who is the disposer of all life,
becomes of value for some purpose of His will.
Even if we have no idea of how it can be used or
how any value can be attached to it, the action of
committing the whole day in all its experience to
God takes from every kind of experience its use-
lessness. The act of recognizing the day as a
separate thing, the end of which is to be glory to
God, makes the day a distinctly new thing with
its own sense of adventure, although our feet have
to tread an old and familiar way.

Naturally most people would wish to follow this
with thanksgiving and prayer for the gift of
friends, our own home folk, and those who are
very often in our thoughts and whose names are
specially dear to us. When one begins a day by
seeking blessing for those we are to meet in the
familiar ways of work or in the unexpected incidents of the day, there is preparation against
those things which hinder friendship and bring
irritation and misunderstandings into life.

The affirmation of faith may take any form

which clearly expresses to ourselves the things on which we stand with most secure trust. The whole of any great Creed may well be used by one to whom each part has its own meaning and truth, even if that meaning be not of common acceptance in the Church. This is not a declaration of faith for public use but a private affirmation of the things most truly believed, and so we are justified in reinterpreting or omitting according to our belief. There are many such affirmations. Each one chooses for himself, and the Scriptures provide glad and confident expressions of assured trust in God, assured even though it sometimes trembles. The purpose of this in such a cell of prayer is to help us to set our feet firmly on the rock of our faith before we go out to meet these forces which tend to draw us away from trust in God and weaken us in the battle of life. We easily forget even treasured things, and it is good to have such definite affirmations and to recall them again and again. In the hour of temptation or need the word that is frequently on our tongue leaps forth to give new strength, or new vision. "I believe in God," "I believe in Jesus Christ," "I believe in the Holy Spirit"; before these, temptations lose much of their power.

The Lord's Prayer is chosen because it comprehends a range of infinite wideness and depth in things which our Lord taught as most essential for man to bring daily to God in prayer.

Probably everyone who reads this would fill up these five minutes in a different way. Even if there were somewhat of the same content it would be expressed quite otherwise.

It is preferable to have a large part of each of these groups of prayers expressed in words which some considerable part of the Church uses, while other parts will be in words of our own individual choice. Even in the very brief occupancy of this cell, of which our own hands have raised the walls, we should seek to realize our union with a great body of those who in past days trusted in God and with those who to-day in our own and other branches of the Church are living in the same trust and using the same words in their prayers. So in the above example the first act of adoration unites the person using it with the communion of Israel, and the words have their meaning deepened by long Christian usage. The words of an ancient Creed unites with the Church of very early days and with those existing branches of the Church to-day, some of which are far separate from us in practice and doctrine, but with whom we are united in this great expression of faith, even if the interpretations differ on this point and on that. So also in the use of the Lord's Prayer we are united with the whole Christian Church, perhaps the only place of our standing together, or rather of our kneeling together, for it is only as we kneel in humbleness and in the poverty of spirit which Christ commands, that we can find ourselves on common ground with every branch of the Church of Christ. Beyond that it unites us with the whole human race in all its need, for " *our* daily bread ", " *our* forgiveness ", " *our* deliverance from evil ", so unites us. There is no stopping-place at which we can say that the " us " for whom we seek goes no farther. When we pray in the spirit of Him who taught the prayer, the " us " embraces all the world for which He died, and all the world that is dear to Him. So in our solitary cell of prayer, as we use the Lord's words, we stretch out one hand to hold that of the entire Church of Christ, and the other to clasp that of the whole world of needy men, beloved of God. This reinforces our prayer.

A definite claim is made for this prepared and, so far as time is concerned, limited act. In every other sense it is not limited and covers the whole range of essential desire. The prayers chosen are the deepest and most unchanging which lie in our hearts, and in their quiet and unhurried offering to God they bring real communion and very great response, and the simple phrases increasingly carry greater meaning and deeper desire. This is

particularly true of the clauses in the Lord's
Prayer, each one of which grows in meaning
through meditative use. There does not seem
much time for response from God in actual guidance, but that comes in ways which are quite
independent of the conditions of time. Even a
dream is able to annul these conditions, much
more surely God's purpose of communion with
man. The deeper and more continuous experience
of this response, however, will be found in the
providences of the day and in the whole action of
God on ourselves, action which reveals itself in
direct guidance, in a changed spirit, in quietness of
mind and new energy of thought and of desire.
What we experience in our lives we also believe is
true for those for whom we make intercession and
for the " us " of the Lord's Prayer.

Beyond this continual benefit and the honour-
ing of God in it, there is the special value spoken
of at the beginning. Such a sequence often makes
prayer possible and strengthening for tired and
over-driven people, when longer prayers and un-
prepared devotions seem impossible. They can
be used when every faculty is dulled by weariness
or when sudden emergencies of time arise. Used
in times of spiritual storm or dryness, in illness, in
travelling, they provide a prepared and familiar
path which entails no mental exertion and yet has

great religious value. They gained this value from their use when the faculties engaged were more fresh and life not so rushed. They keep it unlessened in the day of storm or haste. Not only so, as if knowing that the time of their use will be short, these faculties seem to recover vigour when prayer is renewed in the cell, and they retain the new influx of life during the period of prayer.

If this reinvigoration does not come, and the words become to consciousness only repeated words, without urgency of desire or activity of will, this does not mean that they are useless. They have been chosen as the heart's real desire, as the intellect's real choice, as the will's real purpose, in the active and reverent hour when they were prepared. All this does not go out of life when the mind becomes sleepy and the emotion dull and the will outwearied. Deep in our hearts lies this thing which is our heart's real prayer to God, and the expression by the overwearied life is not mere repetition. It is the actual bringing to God, according to our human capacity at that moment, all the deep desire of our heart and the earnest purpose of our will, and surely God will hear it and accept it according to its reality in our hearts, rather than according to the insufficiency of our utterance and our emotion. Even this, however, does not express all the experience. It will often be found that when the feet are set again on this well-travelled and familiar way of prayer, refreshment comes to the spirit, and life which was weary becomes active and strong again. So also, because in this quiet five minutes there is separation from hurry and entire leisure for all that it is to contain, the sense of leisure clings after the five minutes is over and helps to defy the rush which makes so much of life ineffective.

For many people, perhaps for most, it will be found helpful to have every word of these prayers written out, and the saying of them aloud, even though in a whisper. This does help to fix the mind when it is inclined to wander, but that is not all the value. Words are meant to be said, not just thought, and the sounded word has power to quicken its own meaning. The more tired one is, the more valuable this is. The more active the mind is and the desire, the more sensitive these are to the power of the spoken word.

There are many books of prayers which have a sequence for each day, often wide in range and beautiful in expression. These vary each day for a week or a month. The cell is distinguished from these in three ways. First, by the fact that it does not vary in form; every morning is the same, and each midday and evening has its own unchanging sequence. The tired mind has never to face an unfamiliar idea or emotion. These words are originally chosen with care as the expression of the deepest desire of the heart, the most fixed purpose of the will. Each phrase is a centre to which new experiences and interpretations attach themselves, enriching it. Each is a framework within which a vision of God grows in clearness. There is a continual unfolding and the revealing of new grace and truth, *within the phrase*. It does not need to change its form—every enlarged meaning clings to the familiar word. Look at " let the whole earth be filled with His glory "; or at " let the grace of the Lord Jesus Christ be with them "; or at " give us this day our daily bread ". Reverently and continuously desired and prayed, these become unfolding words, richer in meaning, calling for advance in grace, as they become more laden with the response of God. In the tired or distracted hour, when little seems to remain but the empty phrase, some afterglow of that radiance still rests upon it. It is worth " all that " to God.

A second distinguishing feature is that every cell is built on adoration. If the mind and desire are too weak or disturbed to follow even to the end of five minutes' devotions, here in the first words is set for the vital thing, the mark of everlasting light: GLORY TO GOD. All intercession is in that, all petition is there, all thanksgiving. It draws back to itself everything that follows, even the prayer for the humble day's work or the night's rest. It throws its light forward on everything that is yet to be prayed, as the central desire of all.

The third feature is that the whole thing is either chosen or formed by ourselves, in accordance with our own temperament, our own most real desire and will. It is rare to find continual harmony with our own view of the Divine or of human need in any book of prayers. That is ensured here, and even in the words " chosen ", there is a feeling that they are our own because we ourselves have chosen them.

It is inevitable that some will not find this form of devotion suited to their temperament or mind. It may seem opposed to the more spontaneous and intimate ways of communion with God, which require no such preparation, nor provision for dull and weak seasons, or find that provision by less formal means. No claim is made which would set it against any other way of prayer. The only claim made is that it has actually been helpful to a number who needed such help, and that it seems a common-sense application of well-known facts of the spiritual life.

At the end of one of the wisest books of a past generation on the spiritual life, after giving specific directions as to certain practices of prayer, the

K

writer, Dean Goulburn, uses words which are quoted here in reference to this less full and wise attempt at guidance: " Make experiment of this advice, remembering that in spiritual as in intellectual discipline, early efforts are for the most part clumsy failures, and that repeated trials are the uniform condition of success: and you shall find, under the blessing of God, that your prayers will grow in life and interest, and will give that bright and happy tone to the mind, without which no one ever encountered successfully the duties and temptations of active life."

CHAPTER XIII

WE believe in God immanent in the world and in the affairs of individuals in the world, an immanence manifested in the history of nations and of men, and in prayer we show our belief in a relationship between God and the world which is affected by the prayers of men. We believe that as our mind and affection and will are turned towards God such response comes from Him as deeply affects the character and the movements of these faculties. We believe that with the continuance of prayer throughout the days, these faculties become more sensitive towards God, and therefore more sensitive to all God's action upon the world. Immediately, and with growing power, this greater sensitiveness affects those with whom we are in contact through prayer, and opens doors of entrance for the love of God to reach them. The more closely our desire draws near to the desire of Christ, the more naturally and surely will these doors be opened. The more worthily also will the prayers which have this sensitiveness be named by the name of Christ and asked "in Jesu's name".

The main areas of response may be indexed thus:

1. Quickened faculties and clearer vision.
2. The so-called "happenings" of the day.
3. A sensitive universe.
4. Increased range of Intercession.
5. Direct Guidance. (See next chapter.)
6. Peace of heart and unity of life.
7. Direct "answer" and the experience we call "unanswered prayer" come also into consideration here.

1. Sufficient has been written in previous chapters about the quickening of faculties. These strengthened faculties in turn are directed towards wider and also to more intimate spheres of prayer and receive there still deepened sensitiveness and power. So there is a constant action and reaction between those practices of prayer which are within our power and the divine influence which responds to these human activities.

2. The Daily Providences. Among the many strengthening acts of response from God, and one

which is filled with happiness and interest is that the "happenings" of the day appear in close connection with the prayers that have been made. The outgoings of nature, the social order and disorder, the special incidents of the day, have all an aspect of response for the praying man. No doubt he himself shapes the ways of these providences— "Prepare ye the way of the Lord, make His paths straight"—but the response of God is found on these prepared ways. There is continual response also to the prepared spirit though the way be unseen.

The attitude of watchfulness for response is a far wider thing than mere watchfulness against evil. It brings a new and happy outlook on all life. Often it changes the cause of irritation into a cause of amusement. It brings interest to days that seem dull, even as the geologist finds treasures in what to others seem dead stones. It wakens the soul and the mind to the values of common things and changes many common incidents into wonderful experiences, because they are seen as the responses of God, all whose doings are wonderful.

Here is an instance. One of our morning prayers is for the grace of patience. We know that all virtues are strengthened in dealing with opposition, and from experience we know that God does not usually make a person patient or wise or strong by an immediate gift, but by His sufficient grace in the ordinary struggle of life. Yet in spite of the prayer and in spite of the knowledge, a man may meet the little oppositions of daily life with a ruffled spirit, unmindful of his prayer, and faithless to the grace of humour. A delayed post, a bad breakfast egg, the late arrival of a train, a wet day, some petty irritation, makes him impatient or irritable, and appears as opposition to his prayer, a snare of the devil, where a spirit watchful for response would see in these a sort of comical provision for receiving and improving the grace of patience, and becoming a patient person. There is no need to attach to this the belief that God delays the train, or arranges for the decay of the egg. They are just the ordinary events of the world's happenings, but they are brought out of that into the realm of response through the use which a prayerful spirit enables a man to make of them. The world is full of this kind of humorous or solemn relationship of prayer and event, and it is no sound judgment which refuses to see them as answers because they are there whether the prayer be made or no. The answer is in the mind which associates two otherwise unassociated things, and there is constantly in the general providences of God rich store of answers to

specific requests, even as the Scriptures testify:
"Before they call I will answer, and while they
are yet speaking I will hear."

3. The world becomes sensitive. We know
and feel the world as sensitive to human action
and emotion, and in prayer we become sure that
we are bringing powers of the world to come into
contact with a responsive world. The world
gradually becomes not only transparent but revealing. This may not be noticeable in any one
act of prayer, though to some it comes then in
sudden revelation. Much more commonly it
grows upon us as a developing experience. All
life, the natural world with its beauty, its love, its
terrors, comes into connection with God and reveals Him in some reality of His being and His
working. The course of all history, of Britain
as of Israel, of the present day and hour as of
the past, the common experiences of men, our
personal life, all these become more and more
"spiritually discerned", as St. Paul puts it, and
God appears in them in a measure of self-revela-
tion. He *comes* in them. This is not a claim that
we are led to understand everything in life or
history or nature, nor to arrive at a solution of all
mysteries. It is a claim that we experience and
find in these in response to prayer, a transparency
and clearness which reveals God at the heart of

life, and of history. "The Lord sitteth as King for ever."

4. Along another line of connection there is response. The sphere of Intercession often lies apparently removed from immediate contact with our ordinary life. We pray, for example, that the help of God be given to some conquered or oppressed people in lands and circumstances apparently outside the realm of our help. We offer our prayer, believing that through it God will mediate some direct help, and in deep reality it is given. There is, however, a response beyond the direct blessing for which we pray. To one who consistently is seeking awareness to response there will come knowledge of oppressions in *spheres within his reach*, perhaps oppressions of which he himself is guilty, and in sensitiveness to that vision, he will act.

A mother praying for her son who is far away and out of immediate contact brings blessing to him, but there is a second response to the prayer in awareness of sons of other mothers whom her life can touch with the kindness she seeks for her own. The range of this second response is almost infinite, and it affects every kind of prayer, even personal petition. Ronald Knox, in his own distinctive manner, writes, "Remember that it is only a part even of your most private intercessions which is applied to a special intention : the whole Church of God is benefited when any little girl prays for a new doll." Does that sound non-sensical? It holds a great truth.

6. We often feel the burden of having many things to do, and a distracting number of different things to attend to. There is therefore always something left undone, and the duty undone tires and weighs upon the spirit more than the heaviest task accomplished. In our lives also, there are competing or conflicting motives, higher and lower, and life is distracted by the opposing claims. In many lives there is a constant sense of rush, or worse still, of being driven. In prayer we learn that there is only *one* thing to do. We learn that the Will of God can be done without harassing thought of our own inability : and that He does not seek from us more than time, rightly used, can hold. This is wonderful response; the sense of Unity, the many changed into the One, the one Will, the one Master, and assurance of power given with the command. This brings liberation of faculties and gives discrimination among claims. This reduces now, and perhaps at the last abolishes, the discord in living. If there be bodily or mental weariness, there is not the same nervous exhaustion nor unquiet spirit. The communion with God in life ensures that.

7. It is a right and natural thing that all our speech to God should end with some act of the will in connection with our prayer, thus opening our mind and spirit to any response from Him. That response will be given. Men express this in different ways. One may say, " I listen for the voice of God, and he speaks." Another may say, " As I wait with a willing spirit, ideas coloured by my prayer come into my mind, which seems to be made sensitive by the approach to God. I accept these as the response of God." A third says, " I just go about my business, but I find doors opening, things happening, help given, opportunities given which have direct connection with my prayers, and I accept these as the answer from God." These three, and many more, do not exclude each other, and they all need " acceptance ". That is given first in the act of will which is in our prayer, and it is given in more detail as the word or the idea, or the opportunity comes. Without this acceptance, prayers may easily become meaningless repetitions, and the response of God have no channel along which it can flow into life.

There is a place of prayer in which there seems often no response. Our prayers are clearly in agreement with the Will of God who gave His own Son to redeem men from sin, when we pray for the characters and the salvation of our children, of husband or wife, of brother or sister or dear friend. Yet sometimes men pray year after year, and what is asked is not granted and the prayers seem to effect nothing. These lives go on as if prayer had never been made, and yet Christ said, " If ye shall ask anything in My name, I will do it." Men have prayed till their lives passed away in prayer, and those they prayed for have died in the old shame or sin.

Often we blame ourselves when our prayers seem to effect nothing, and deplore our lack of faith, or love, or persistence. That is too shallow a reasoning, and it changes the emphasis of " saving grace " to our prayers rather than to God's love.

Christ Himself has just this same experience: Christ who speaks these words to us, " If ye shall ask anything in My name, I will do it." Christ Himself has this to bear. " He came unto His own, and they that were His own received Him not." Prayer and desire were His life: most loving desire. " How often would I have gathered thee! " That was not the cry of an hour but of every beat of His heart. The prayer He taught us was the breath of His own life—" Hallowed be Thy Name: Thy Kingdom come: Thy will be done on earth as it is in heaven." Two thousand years have passed of that prayer, never ceasing on earth and in the eternal intercessions of heaven. What is the state of earth to-day?

This Saviour Christ bears on His heart all the names that are in our prayer; our sons or daughters, our husbands, our wives, brothers, sisters, lovers, beloved. *As God deals with our prayers for these dear ones He deals with the prayer and the sacrifice of Christ for these same beloved names.* Christ is with us in this place of waiting. He is making our prayer His own continually when our prayer is for salvation for anyone. We may have reason to think *our* prayer can meet no granting of request: but what when Christ makes it His? "If ye shall ask anything in My name, I will do it."

So we come back to His word, "I will do it"— but it is not always done. No, under the present conditions of time and place it is not always done. So many of the offers of God are like that, even the promise of His coming. We fall back on something other than this present experience. What have we to trust to? We have the promise of Christ, repeated so often: we have the eternal and sufficient sacrifice of Christ, the prayer embodied in the Cross of Calvary: we have the eternal intercession of Christ who ever liveth to make intercession: we have the prevailing love of God for sinners, which Christ makes known.

Here in these prayers for dear ones we are face to face with the ultimate mystery of created life, the mystery of the human soul standing before his Creator, living and moving in Him, sustained by Him and dependent on Him for every breath, and yet free to defy the Will of God, and free to resist the love poured out in prayer and sacrifice by God and man. There lies over that free created soul the righteousness of God, vast and patient and omnipotent like an eternal decree, from which no man can escape, justifying the apostolic language of election and foreknowledge and fore-ordination : and there lies over that free created soul the love that accepts no defeat and knows no failure offering Himself in sacrifice for His own creatures.

We do not know what it all means—the present delay and contradictions. We do not know the steps by which that constraining righteousness will draw these souls to Him. We do not know the future on this side, or beyond the grave, but we commit our wandering and dear friends to Him. " I know whom I have believed, and am persuaded that He is able to keep that I have committed unto Him against that day."

CHAPTER XIV

DIVINE GUIDANCE

> " I go to prove my soul!
> I see my way as birds their trackless way.
> I shall arrive! what time, what circuit first
> I ask not: but unless God sends His hail
> Or blinding fireballs, sleet or stifling snow,
> In some time, His good time, I shall arrive:
> He guides me and the bird. In His good time! "
> —Browning's *Paracelsus*.

THE following scheme for thought about guidance needs little explanation. I have found it helpful to have the matter stated in compressed tabular form. In the last few years there has been increased debate about the guidance of God and how it may be secured. I do not propose to discuss the many varying theories, but to set down one set of principles which seem to be in agreement with Scripture, and with experience.

STUDY SCHEME ON DIVINE GUIDANCE

1. *Fundamental Conditions*
    1. "We must be travelling the same road as our guide."

2. "We must habitually seek guidance and watch for it."

3. "We must habitually follow the guidance given."

2. *The Fact of Divine Guidance*

   1. Attested and assumed by the whole Scripture record.

   2. Promised by Jesus Christ.

   3. Experienced by the Church, both in ways opened and ways stopped.

   4. Proved by human experience, as recorded in a great mass of biography and by our own personal history, and in the ordinary events of life.

These indicate the Outer Media for Divine Guidance.

3. *Inner Media for Divine Guidance*

   1. Reason, plan, judgment, common sense.

   2. Imagination, emotion, primitive instincts.

   3. Conscience, and the sense of Duty, "The daughter of the Voice of God".

4. In all the above there is the needed interpretation of the Holy Spirit, and beyond these named there are special occasions when messages from God seem to come *in independence of any human faculty*. There is an indefinable "awareness" of things to be done or of a way to be taken.

Section 1

1. The "fundamental conditions" are taken, not quite literally, from Miss Caroline Stephen's *Vision of Faith*.

Miss Stephen was a Quaker, and there is in the literature of the Society of Friends very abundant and gracious teaching on this subject. The three conditions are obviously fundamental, yet obviously they are often unheeded. Good people not infrequently seek God's guidance for some doubtful enterprise, and the selfishness in life is apt to invade our prayers and affect these conditions. Beyond that, in the more superstitious realms of life, there is much conscious and unconscious violation of these conditions. A gambler prays that he may be guided to choose the right card or horse. A student who has neglected his work and is unfitted for his profession will yet pray that he may have guidance to pass-answers in his examinations. There are prayers for guidance in the strategy of war. We all know many instances. We have all felt the temptation. (We all know in person the trespassing schoolboy who prays that God will keep the dog quiet while he climbs the apple tree!) We probably have all made prayers we would not care to reveal, so far are they from the mind of Christ. They are cries of the unrighteous heart's desire in a life struggling towards God.

There is much Divine Guidance in lives that do not observe these conditions, restraining and saving while men are on the wrong road and following the wrong guide. There is light that comes to those who are not seeking and to those who are living in disobedience. This is the mercy of God which is ever seeking men in their wandering, and in pity saving and delivering, but for "a guided life" these three conditions are fundamental. We must walk on the same way as our Guide.

2. In the Book of Proverbs, Chapter II, wisdom and discernment are promised to those who cry after them and lift up the voice for them, who seek as for silver and search as for hid treasure. To those, it is said that they will understand every good path. The New Testament does not cancel this requirement: "Ask, seek, knock", is the threefold counsel Christ gives (Luke xi. 10). Habitual guidance comes to habitual seeking; occasional guidance may follow occasional search. God is ever seeking to guide, but without the attitude of man's spirit which is sensitive to His communication, the thrust of His spirit is not perceived as it is by one who consistently seeks and watches. This sensitiveness develops through regular humble seeking which notes the signs,

and Divine guidance directs life—life, not only "events" in life.

3. We must habitually follow the guidance given. Here something is added to the last requirement, not asking and watching alone, but steady obedience. All the faculties of perception are dulled unless this habitual obedience keeps them bright, and habitual disobedience in one matter, spreads a mist over the whole. There is no such thing as an act of disobedience "in itself". It rests on a state of life and represents something which is not incidental but has its place in the soul.

"Take heed, dear Friends, to the promptings of love and truth in your hearts, which are the leadings of the Holy Spirit of God. Resist not His strivings within you. It is His light that shows us our darkness and leads to true repentance. It is God's love that draws us to Him, a redemptive love shown forth in Jesus Christ in all His life and, above all, on the Cross. He is the Way, the Truth, the Life." (Quaker Advices.)

Section 2

Five great and common channels through which God sends His guidance are noted here, and these also affirm the fact of Guidance. We seek in prayer the guidance of God: these are

some of the guides He gives. They may easily
be unrecognized and the guidance missed. The
guidance they convey may be taken, sometimes
indeed it is forced on us and yet the fact of guidance not be recognized, its connection with our
prayers be missed and our gratitude to God be
lacking.

1. With great constancy the Scriptures flash
light upon the life of the watchful reader. They
reach intimate personal life with the restraining
word or the delivering message, "Living, and
active, and sharper than any two-edged sword, and
piercing even to the dividing of soul and spirit,
of both joints and marrow, and quick to discern
the thoughts and intents of the heart." (Heb.
iv. 12.) This applies to the Scriptures just as
we have them to-day, and the word is true to
Christian experience. *They enter life.* "There
is a certain harmony between the Scriptures and
the experience of those who are walking in the
truth which causes them constantly to throw light
one upon the other." So says Dr. Rendel Harris.
It is easy to test how true that is.

To follow what was once a common custom,
opening the Bible at random, in hope that some
verse may stand out for guidance, is quite
irrational. Our regular reading, however, is in
a book of such spiritual quality and width of

application that we are never likely to miss finding in it light for the day's walking.

2. Faith in God's guidance for blundering and
imperfect men who sought to know His will, was
a foundation of peace in the heart of Jesus as He
left the company of believers in the darkening
world. He reiterated it in the last days as if by
assuring the disciples He would assure also His
own heart. "When He, the spirit of truth, is
come, He shall guide you into all the truth."
"You shall know the truth and the truth shall
make you free." "Behold, I send you forth as
sheep in the midst of wolves, be ye therefore wise
as serpents and harmless as doves . . . when they
deliver you up, be not anxious how or what ye
shall speak: for it shall be given you in that hour
what ye shall speak." The word "guidance" is
not used by our Lord, but the fact and promise
of guidance is often on His lips, "I will not leave
you alone: I will come to you."

3. This guidance was experienced by the early
Church. There are a few verses in the book of
Acts which sum up what seems to have been the
daily life of the Church. "And they (Paul and
Timothy) went through the region of Phrygia and
Galatia, *having been forbidden of the Holy Ghost*
to speak the word in Asia; and . . . they assayed
to go into Bithynia; and the *spirit of Jesus suffered*

them not." Then follows the vision, or dream, of the appealing "man of Macedonia". "And when he (Paul) had seen the vision, straightway we sought to go forth into Macedonia, *concluding that God had called us* for to preach the Gospel unto them." (Acts xvi. 5-10.) (Notice the element of interpretation by reason here.) That passage represents the faith and the experience of the early Church in its daily life. Every branch of the Church to-day claims such guidance for its activities, its extension and progress. It is doubtful if the same claim is or can be made for its inertia. This so often has another source.

4. Perhaps it is peculiarly a privilege of older years to see with clearness how fully " guidance " affects our own daily life. Certainly there is a larger area of life to look over. Age may see as guidance what youth may see as frustration, and it is able to judge the whole life-guidance more than by episodes. Judgments made in the midst of an experience are not always so wise as the judgments made when the fruit of the experience has ripened. What Quarles wrote about the doings of the world has wisdom for the judging of our own experience.

> " My soul, sit thou a patient looker-on,
>   Judge not the play before the play is done,
>   Her plot hath many changes; every day
>   Speaks a new scene; *the last act crowns the play.*"

" We deduce a doctrine of guidance," says Rendal Harris, " from the fact of being led." That is true, even where in event after event we seem at the hour to be left to the driving forces of the world. The world is in God's hand, and we are not left unguided.

Ordinary human life is built on a sacramental basis, and conveys God's guidance. Pascal speaks of " The Orders of God's Holy Providence ", a noble thought and one which takes away much of our discontent. We may think of ourselves as helpless powers in the game of life, moved by forces over which we have no control, or we can take hold of the changes of life or its monotony, as guidance from God, calling us to acceptance or resistance or direction of circumstances so that they bring glory to God and help to man. He who will walk in the latter way will find common life to be very sentient of God. Changes, events, circumstances, and all that men call good luck and bad luck become " Providences ", the pointing of God's finger, the direction of God's Will. Life is full of these, even the most monotonous life. " He that will mark Providences, will never lack for Providences to mark," said a Quaker saint.

" Ye are the light," says Christ. The worth of human example, inspiring us to higher thought and life, is beyond reckoning, as it comes to us in personal contacts and in the great biographies. Our first and our right thought of God's guidance as coming through noble men and women is true to Christ's word, " Ye are the light of the world." There is no need to emphasize that, but we should note that guidance comes also from spheres where perhaps some of us have not seen it. *The need of men is one of the common and authoritative guides of life.* It called and guided our Lord and directed His steps, the need of evil, broken men. Man's sin guided Him to the cross. The sorrow of Martha and Mary led Him to Bethlehem. It was certainly His spirit of love which led Him, but the outer medium was the need of sinful humanity. It is still so for followers of this same Lord, and we find in the loss and the sin and the need of man guidance for our steps into ways dark or bright, constant or occasional, which are the paths of God's choice for us.

If any of us lives a somewhat sheltered or re-stricted life there may be need for insight on another way of guidance and revelation which comes from those whom in our narrowness we may call " bad " people. Bad as they may be, there are few whose lives may not bring to us some teaching or revelation or guidance concerning our view of God, and the direction of our thought and action.

Here are words of a wise Christian poet, Evelyn Underhill:

" Thy naughty ones, rebellious, cunning, adventurous,
Breaking the toys of their brothers, thrusting their
    tortuous lives athwart the respectable web—
These too!
Do these not exhibit Thy vigour, Thy rude inexhaustible
    freedom,
Correcting with flushes of passion our colourless pictures
of God.

(The Likeness, v. 5.)

To one who seeks for guidance, it comes through all sorts of avenues. It may not come along the line of careful thought, it may not come while one prays, but a book picked up in an idle moment or a street scene or the word of a song, will bring the message and may bring it with a very imperative voice. " The Spirit of Jesus giveth life," and " the life is the light of men ". Guidance is very sure and the whole area of life's experience is used as a medium for it. This guidance, whether of check or goad, or reproach or praise, this voice of the Master in the heart, is one of the supreme facts of life for the man who prays.

Section 3

In the realm of immediate guidance we reach the higher levels of communion with God, and there also we are using faculties which are misleading if there is not sincere obedience. We use the powers of thought, judgment, common sense which God had given us, in searching for the best uses of life and of the situation of the day. We plan and arrange our living on the result of that search, not making our plan a chain on freedom but an incitement to steady progress. God has given us brains for that end.

We use our faculties of imagination by which we are able to put ourselves in a brother's place, to enter into situations different from our own, to see in the common life of the streets and in common people and common circumstances somewhat of what God sees and yearns over and loves. Imagination is a main channel for guidance in the Holy Spirit. So we can visualize an ideal, and then apply our more pedestrian powers of thought and judgment to bring the ideal into earthly form, to "build Jerusalem, in England's green and pleasant land". The man who never sees or builds castles in the air will never build mansions of worth on the earth. In our own limited way we are all artists and poets, and musicians, and the gift which they have in special measure is ours also for our guidance. It reaches its highest point in the vision of God. Moses endured "as seeing Him who is invisible". The saints tell of the wonder of the beatific vision. Very common folk, still battling against evil and often cast down, can find in prayer and life such a sense of God's presence and such indications of His Will as give assurance that the Guide is with us and that He leads men still.

Our emotions are a channel for God's guidance. All through the Scriptures that is prominent. " And being moved with compassion " is a frequent thought in the Gospels, and our Lord's pity, and sympathy, and wonder, and indignation are set forth as guiding and determining His actions. As guides for us they have a value additional to the clear light which reason gives. They draw and woo us, and lead us with a glow in our hearts where reason alone would make dull and toilsome travelling.

Conscience is generally recognized as the medium through which God guides men, and it is often exalted above reason and imagination and emotion. When exalted to a level where these faculties are criticized as giving a less certain " Voice of God ", conscience may deceive men. No faculty is more open to misleading influences. Yet this mysterious authority, so dominating and yet so corruptible, is an outstanding voice of guidance. It allies itself readily with that sense of Duty, the " Daughter of the Voice of God " in

Hebrew phrase, which adds to vision of the way an imperative command to walk in it.   Should any reader not know Wordsworth's " Ode to Duty ", I counsel a careful study of it, as adding to the idea of conscience, something which carries its imperative voice beyond the sphere of moral right and wrong into that of courage and peace and joy, with wooing harmonies.

" Stern Daughter of the Voice of God!
  O Duty! if that name thou love
  Who art a light to guide, a rod
  To check the erring, and reprove;
  Thou, who art victory and law
  When empty terrors overawe;
  From vain temptations dost set free;
  And calm'st the weary strife of frail humanity."

It is a strange thing that the primitive instincts, hunger and thirst, love and passion and social instincts should be so much ignored in religious books, except as voices which misguide.   Give them a place, these fundamental and overwhelming urges of flesh and spirit, not of flesh alone. Very corruptible, yes!   So is conscience, so is the sense of duty—to what atrocities have these led men!   So is the whole range of reason and judgment and emotion and imagination.   Very corruptible.   They all need to be brought into subjection to Christ if they are not to lead us wrong, but asked humbly, each has its own special light and guidance to yield. It is no proof of wisdom when the subjection to Christ of our primitive instincts is changed into blindness to the light and deafness to the word which comes through the very constitution of our humanity. Life will be more natural and free when these are given their proper place among the media of guidance, under the purifying power of Christ.

The whole of life is used by God to convey to us His Will and His Light. Through every part the Holy Spirit speaks. Other voices speak, voices of deceit, voices of the pit. These two make claims to guide life, and issue imperative demands. It is as life becomes sensitive to the voice of God, the gift He gives to those who seek Him, that discrimination grows in wisdom. These others become the "voice of strangers" whose powers to woo and claims to direct grow less and less as we obey the supreme word. There is a Holy Spirit, and as we bring life humbly to His judgment the corruptible elements in our lives are purified. The words Bunyan spoke to Conscience are truthful, not for conscience alone, but for all human faculty and instinct, from the deepest reason to the most primitive hunger.

"Mr. Conscience, although I have made thee a minister and a preacher to the town of Mansoul, yet as to the things which the Lord Secretary (the Holy Spirit) knoweth and shall teach to this people there thou must be a scholar and a learner, even as the rest of Mansoul are." *(The Holy War.)*

CHAPTER XV

CONCLUSION of Tertullian's Treatise on Prayer, written at the close of the second century, A.D.[1]

"Christian prayer furnishes with patience those who suffer and feel and grieve, it supplements grace with valour. Consequently it avails to recall the souls of the departed from the pathway of death, to recover the weak, to heal the sick, to exorcise the dæmoniacs, to open the gates of the prison, to loose the bonds of the innocent. This it is that washes away sins, repels temptations, quenches persecutions, consoles the weak-hearted, delights the great-spirited, brings back travellers, stills the waves, stupefies brigands, nourishes the poor, rules the rich, directs the sick, raises the lapsed, upholds the falling, sustains the standing.

"Prayer is the wall of faith, our armour and our weapons against the enemy who watches us on

[1] The translation is taken with grateful acknowledgment from Dr. Bindley s *St. Cyprian on the Lord's Prayer* (S.P.C.K.).

every side. Therefore let us never walk unarmed.
By day let us be mindful of our station, by night
of our vigil.   Under the arms of prayer let us
guard the standard of our Captain, in prayer let
us await the trumpet of the angel.   Even the
angels all pray.   Every creature prayeth.   The
cattle and wild beasts pray and bend their knees,
and as they go forth from their stalls and caves
look up to Heaven, not with silent mouth, making
their breath vibrate after their own manner. Even
the birds as they soar from their nest strain
towards heaven, stretching out the cross of their
wings for hands, and utter what may well be a
prayer.

" *What more, then, of the duty of prayer?   The
Lord Himself prayed—to Whom be honour and
power for ever and ever.*"